# GUNS OVER THE CAROLINAS
## The Story of Nathanael Greene

# By the Same Author

Ralph Edgar Bailey

# GUNS OVER THE CAROLINAS
## The Story of Nathanael Greene

Maps by James MacDonald
Frontispiece by Franz Altschuler

William Morrow and Company        New York 1967

JB  G-83 B
c,2

To G. E. B.

★

# Maps

# Contents

# 1

## Rhode Island Boy
★ ★ ★ ★ ★ ★ ★ ★ ★ ★ ★ ★ ★ ★

When Nathanael Greene was born in Potowomut, Rhode Island, on July 27, 1742, a Quaker astrologer prophesied that he would be "a great man." That the boy would have to achieve greatness in spite of a serious physical handicap and the lack of formal education was no part of the prophecy.

Nathanael Greene, the elder, was a famous anchor smith, gristmill operator, proprietor of a general store, and part-time Quaker preacher. He conceded that each of his sons ought to know how to read, write, and cipher; he himself had needed such a rudimentary education to manage the extensive family business. But he both feared and despised book learning.

The elder Nathanael was well able to afford an education for his sons. His ownership of three forges and a gristmill adjoining the comfortable, rambling old homestead set on a hill that sloped gently down to the little Potowomut River made him one of the most affluent citizens of the colony of Rhode Island. And he owned another forge, gristmill, and store in Coventry, on the Pawtuxet River, ten miles to the north. He was a kind and just man, within his lights, but he was superstitious, and he lived by a stern and uncompromising code.

Nathanael Greene, the younger, showed early in life that he was different from the other sons, five brothers and two stepbrothers, all of whom were content to live as their father dictated. Despite the handicap of a limp in his right leg caused by a stiff knee, a birth defect, he could outrun, outjump and outwrestle any other boy his age in Kent County. And he could swing a heavy sledge hammer all day at the anvil in the forge, shaping the famous Greene ship's anchors. But, as much as he loved all forms of outdoor exercise, sports were not his only pastime. He read the Bible and such of the few other standard books of the day of which his father approved, then asked for more. Soon he ran squarely up against his father's unrelenting aversion to book learning. He argued so persistently and so persuasively, however, that at last his father relented to the extent of hiring, for a brief period, a man named Maxwell to tutor the boy in East Greenwich. But this little learning only fired Nathanael Greene's determination to know more. Mathematics particularly fascinated him.

When the elder Nathanael flatly refused to pay good money to buy books for his son, young Nathanael quickly worked out a scheme to make himself independent of his father's prejudices. He began, quite openly, to fashion small anchors and other toys made of iron in his spare time. As he expected, he found a ready market for them in Newport, to which thriving town he often sailed in the little sloop *Two Brothers* with a cargo of anchors and flour. Newport, at the entrance to Narragansett Bay, in those days was one of the most important seaports in North America. It had a population of 11,000, and a harbor that almost always was filled comfortably with shipping.

Nathanael Greene's first purchase with the money his toys brought was an expensive volume of Euclid, bound in dark sheepskin. He was extremely proud of it and carried it with him almost everywhere—even at the forge and mill—working out problems in geometry.

Nathanael Greene made many trips down the bay to Newport over the years, and on most of them, stowed carefully aboard the little craft, along with the cargo, was a small canvas bag containing his homemade iron toys. As he sold them he purchased more books—the writings of Seneca, Horace, the Latin poets, Locke, Swift, and those of other well-known authors. Soon he put up a book shelf in his bedroom over the kitchen ell in the tree-shaded homestead.

Perhaps the elder Nathanael at last may have taken a secret pride in the ambition and accomplishments of his fourth son and namesake. At least, he made no further objections to the boy's studying, and he never seemed to begrudge the small amounts of valuable iron that were used in making the toys. Perhaps, too, he remembered the prophecy made at the boy's birth. But on one point the elder Nathanael was uncompromisingly firm. Much as his son loved to dance, this activity still was a strictly forbidden pleasure. Nathanael Greene, however, was just as determined to have fun as to obtain the fundamentals of an education. So he climbed out of his bedroom window at night onto a conveniently overhanging maple limb, shinnied down the tree trunk, and walked to East Greenwich or to one of the neighboring farms to enjoy himself at a dance or a husking bee.

Once, when he was fifteen, Greene found his father waiting for him with a horsewhip on his return from a dance. The whipping that followed probably was well deserved, since he deliberately had disobeyed his father, but it proved rather less painful than might have been expected. For, anticipating ultimate discovery, young Nathanael had hidden a half dozen wooden shingles in a convenient place. Quickly he shoved them under his outer clothing before facing his angry father. The shingles, of course, took the brunt of the beating. And perhaps too, the elder Nathanael didn't lay on the whip quite as hard as he might have.

There were other dances and other husking bees as the years passed, and Nathanael Greene attended most of them, but his father, for some reason, never again laid a hand on him. Despite his stern Quaker upbringing, the anchor smith may have come to realize that his gifted son needed some form of relaxation after a hard day's work at the forge or gristmill, or after long hours of reading and study.

Nathanael Greene was fond of the society of girls, and apparently, he always knew how to entertain them. He was a big boy, even in his mid-teens, with strongly built shoulders, a full chest, and vigorous limbs. His features were sharply defined; his forehead was high. The mouth was deep at the corners and the lips full, indicating a strong will and a great capacity for the keen enjoyment of life. But there was, too, a trace of tenderness in his expression. Seldom was he other than cheerful, even under trying circumstances.

By 1760, when Nathanael Greene was eighteen, the Greene property was extensive. The business had belonged to the family for four generations, the sons taking only a frugal living as their share. Then Greene's stepbrothers, Benjamin and Thomas, died, and a lawsuit resulted over the disposal of their inheritance. To Nathanael, as the one member of the family with some book learning, fell the not unpleasant task of gathering evidence in the long legal battle to keep the Greene family fortune intact. The lawsuit finally was won by the six surviving brothers, Nathanael, Jacob, William, Elihu, Christopher, and Perry, and their father, but meanwhile Nathanael Greene found himself in a newer, wider, and much more interesting world than that of "the place of all the fires," as the Narragansett Indians called Potowomut Neck.

The legal assignment meant that Nathanael had to begin reading law. Blackstone, then the best authority on the principles of English law, soon became almost as familiar to him as his long cherished volume of Euclid. He met lawyers, judges, clerks of the courts, not only in Rhode Island but in New York and Connecticut. On one trip to New York Greene had himself inoculated against smallpox, at a time when the laws of Rhode Island forbade such immunization. The process left him with a slight blemish in his right eye, but he considered it a small price to pay for protection from this dread disease.

# 2

## Belle of Block Island
★ ★ ★ ★ ★ ★ ★ ★ ★ ★ ★ ★ ★ ★

Nathanael Greene took over management of the forge and gristmill in Coventry in 1770, the year before his father died, and carried on the combined business with his brothers. Before long he built an eight-room house for himself, somewhat resembling the old homestead at Potowomut, but much more elaborate and comfortable, and he included a library in it. Like the home in which he had lived until he was twenty-seven, the new house was set on the brow of a low hill, the land sloping to the little river that supplied the water power to run the forge and mill. More than one hundred families were dependent upon the business for a living.

Nevertheless, Nathanael Greene found time to take his first plunge into public affairs. Aside from his business, nothing interested him as much as education, and he was the first to advocate the establishment of a public school system in Coventry. Under his insistent prodding and persuasive argument, the hard-fisted neighbors finally yielded, and a school was set up and a teacher hired.

The following year, in 1771, he somewhat reluctantly ran for membership in the Rhode Island General Assembly, was elected, and served in that lawmaking body almost continuously until 1775. Greene's principal activity during his service in the Assembly was to help to rewrite the militia laws. All of the colonies in those days depended for their defense upon militiamen, who enlisted for very short periods, sometimes as brief as a few weeks. The laws had not been changed since the early days of Indian fighting.

As he became more experienced, Greene acquired a good style of writing, barring certain errors of grammar and spelling. He wrote rapidly and concisely, and he chose his words with sound judgment. He had the happy faculty of breaking down a problem into its component parts, then, having solved each minor problem, of putting the whole together again. And he was able to impart his findings clearly to those to whom his letters were addressed. During these years he was a busy correspondent.

Greene's keen humor and quick temper were proverbial among those who knew him. He was perhaps a little too quick to resent a fancied insult, but at all times he was master of himself. His bearing was dignified and self-possessed rather than easy or graceful. At one time a young dancing partner remarked, "You dance stiffly, Nathanael." Replying with good humor, more amused than hurt by the comment, he said, "Very true, my dear, but you see that I dance strong."

One evening, in 1773, Greene attended a dance at the big manor house of his cousin, William Greene, just over the Warwick line in East Greenwich. There he met Catherine Littlefield, an orphan. She was the ward of William Greene's wife, who had been Catherine Ray of Block Island. Caty Littlefield, as he soon came to call her, was small, with blue-gray eyes, and vivacious. A graceful dancer, she possessed a lively wit and contributed brightly to the repartee at any social gathering. The courtship proceeded swiftly and smoothly, Greene frequently sailing his little sloop down Narragansett Bay and out to Block Island, where Caty spent part of the year. She was nineteen, he thirty, but the difference in ages did not seem to matter. There were gay parties on the island, and Greene found himself as popular there as on the mainland, chiefly because of his genial nature and amusing talk. On July 20, 1774, Nathanael Greene and Catherine Littlefield were married in the big room of the William Greene mansion, with the future governor himself giving the bride away. The wedding was the biggest social event Kent County had known in a generation. The young couple rode to Coventry, a few miles over the hills, to the new home near the forge and mill and settled down. There they led a quiet country life, sometimes highlighted by social affairs or riding horseback over the countryside.

For more than half a century, until 1764 the citizens of England's thirteen colonies had taxed themselves through their colonial legislatures, spending their own money as they saw fit. But in that year, following the close of the French and Indian War, Great Britain, staggering under a debt of six hundred million dollars—a huge sum in those days—changed her policy. Parliament passed the Sugar Act, attempting thus to compel the American colonies to help pay the cost of the war that had given Britain an empire in North America. The tax on molasses from the West Indies hit all the colonies hard.

"Taxation without representation is tyranny," thundered James Otis of Massachusetts, sounding a battle cry of protest. The American colonists would have none of the sugar tax, and Parliament was forced to repeal the act before it fairly got to work.

There followed, with increasingly loud protests and sometimes strong retaliatory action by the colonies, a

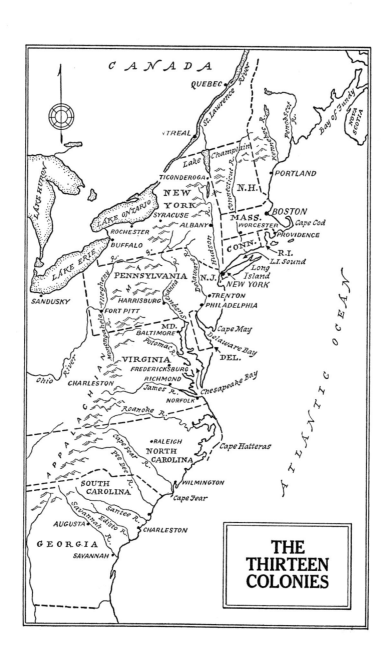

THE
THIRTEEN
COLONIES

series of parliamentary acts including the Quartering Act, by which Boston was forced to house and feed British troops, and the Stamp Act in 1765, requiring revenue stamps for many articles of commerce. This last measure brought forth a ringing denunciation from Patrick Henry, in Virginia, and formation of the Sons of Liberty. There was a notable and profitable increase in smuggling, especially in Boston and Providence. More taxation followed in 1767, with the so-called Townshend Acts, and more troops for police duty were sent to Boston.

On March 5, 1770, there occurred a clash between British Redcoats and citizens on the snow-covered waterfront of Boston in which six Americans were killed. A new British tax on tea led to the burning of the British customs schooner *Gaspee* as she lay aground in Providence harbor on the night of June 9, 1772, and the Boston Tea Party in which an East India Company's ship's whole cargo of nearly 350 chests of tea was dumped by patriots dressed as Indians into Boston harbor in the night of December 16, 1773.

A new Quartering Act was passed by parliament, compelling Boston residents to house British troops not only in barracks and storehouses, but in private homes. An Administration of Justice Act protected Crown officials from interference and revenge by Massachusetts citizens. And on May 13, 1774, General Thomas Gage arrived in Boston to take over command. He was an amiable man with an American wife and had served for a long time in America. But Gage also was a soldier sworn to do his duty, and he practically took over the government of the colony. The parliamentary retaliatory Boston Port Bill, effective on June 8, 1774, tightly closed the port of Boston, bringing sea trade to a halt and threatening to starve the inhabitants.

Nathanael Greene was excited when he heard what George Washington of Virginia had said at Mount Vernon: "I will raise a thousand men, subsist them at my own expense, and march myself at their head to the relief of Boston."

Something indeed had to be done to help the citizens of Boston. The First Continental Congress was formed, composed of representatives from all the thirteen colonies. Committees of Public Safety were organized in each colony. Jacob Greene, one of Nathanael's brothers, was a member of the Rhode Island committee. The Rhode Island General Assembly almost constantly was wrestling with increasing problems connected with the growing tension. And nowhere in North America—not even in Massachusetts—did resentment run higher against King George III and the English parliament.

Arms and ammunition and other supplies of war were being stored rapidly in safe places. Militia laws were rewritten, and new militia companies were organized. In Rhode Island, cannon from British fortifications were stolen one night from Fort Island, and similar moves were carried out in other colonies. Militiamen began drilling on village greens.

The British parliament and the ministry of Frederick Lord North, their anger now at white heat, retaliated by passing the Fisheries Act. It closed the Newfoundland Banks to colonial fishermen. This law, if enforced, would cripple all the colonies.

Nathanael Greene, as a businessman, was deeply affected by almost all of the punitive measures of parliament. And, as a close student of history and of military tactics, he had been watching the events of the past eleven years with growing anxiety. As American merchant shipping suffered, demand for Greene anchors fell off. This loss of business was something personal the British had done to him. He was convinced at last that the colonies would have to declare their independence and set up their own government. And he openly said so, at a time when few men dared to express themselves in public.

On his not infrequent trips to Boston, sixty miles north of his Coventry home, Greene often discussed with his friend Henry Knox, the book seller, the mounting friction between Great Britain and her American colonies. Greene and Knox shared a common belief that war with Great Britain was inevitable, and each was preparing for it in his own way. Greene added the writings of Caesar and Hannibal and some of the more modern European strategists and tacticians such as Turenne, the great French marshal of the seventeenth century, to his library, while Knox delved deeply into the study of the most recent books from London on artillery. Through Knox, Greene met Samuel Adams, the firebrand Boston lawyer, and Paul Revere, the silversmith. They and others were actively preparing for a showdown with England.

"The ministry of Great Britain seem to be determined to imbrue their cursed hands in American blood," Greene wrote to Knox as the ever-mounting quarrel continued to boil.

Threat of an impending clash at arms soon aroused Greene to an active, as well as literary, interest in military affairs. He and his cousin, Griffin Greene, rode over to neighboring Plainfield, Connecticut, one Sunday to participate in a maneuver of militiamen. This act was in deliberate and open defiance of the strict rules of the Quaker sect in which they had been reared. As a result both young men were "read out of the meeting" in East Greenwich.

Thereafter, Greene's participation in military affairs was open and vigorous. He was one of the founders, in 1774, of a company of militia in East Greenwich known as the Kentish Guards, so named for the county in which the town is located. Many of the members of the Kentish Guards wanted Nathanael Greene to be first lieutenant, but a majority objected on the ground that a man with so pronounced a limp should not serve as an officer. One of Greene's close friends, James Mitchell Varnum, a young Boston attorney who had settled in East Greenwich, threatened with others to resign, but yielded to Greene's pleas and accepted the captaincy of the company. Greene was content to remain a private. Everyone else owned a musket, and he must possess one if he were to serve actively, so he rode to Boston to buy a weapon secretly, risking heavy punishment if the British authorities caught him in possession of the firearm. While in Boston, with the help of Knox, he hired a deserting British sergeant to go down to East Greenwich and drill the Kentish Guards.

# 3

## From Anchor Smith to General
★★★★★★★★★★★★★★

Word of the battles of Lexington and Concord reached
Nathanael Greene just before midnight on April 19, 1775,
at his home in Coventry. Neighbors from Massachusetts
to Rhode Island had spread the word by mounted courier,
farm to farm, village to village.

Greene saddled a horse, kissed Caty good-bye, and rode
to East Greenwich to take his place as a private in the
ranks of the Kentish Guards. At daybreak the company
marched for Providence, fourteen miles north, with handsome, brilliant Captain James Mitchell Varnum at their
head.

When the Tory Royal Governor Joseph Wanton in

Newport sent a peremptory order, the Kentish Guards turned back at the Pawtucket line. But Nathanael Greene, two of his brothers, and three other men, borrowing horses, pushed on for Boston, despite the royal governor's command. They turned back when they heard of the stumbling retreat of the Redcoats to Boston.

Three days later the Rhode Island General Assembly in Providence named two commissioners to arrange with Connecticut for a common defense. Nathanael Greene was one of them. Meanwhile, the members of the legislature set about raising a brigade of 1500 troops. Unanimously Greene was elected as brigadier general, and he was commissioned on May 8. Two other men had refused the commission. Greene's dry comment on being told of his election was that "since the Episcopalian and the Congregationalist won't, I suppose the Quaker must."

Greene hated war and all the suffering that inevitably comes in its wake even more than most men because of his upbringing. But he felt there came a time when a man had to take a stand. He wrote to his beloved Caty that he was called forth "to defend our common rights, and repel the bold invaders of the sons of freedom. The cause is the cause of God and man." He had been married less than a year. His private affairs were turned over to Jacob and his other brothers, for Christopher too, was going to war.

Why the legislature elected Greene, with only six months' military experience as a private in the Kentish

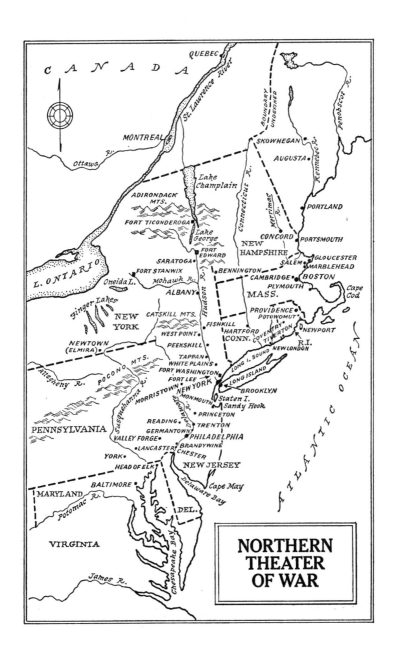

NORTHERN
THEATER
OF WAR

Guards, to be commander of Rhode Island's troops in the
field is not quite clear. Perhaps former Governor Samuel
Ward of Westerly had something to do with the choice.
But more probably Greene's fellow legislators had been
impressed by his solid qualities of leadership, his fertile
imagination, and his aptitude for quick improvisation in
emergencies. They knew, too, that he was the only military scholar in the colony, and one of the very few in any
of the colonies. They probably felt that he could fit theory
to practice.

The Rhode Island brigade of 1500 troops reached
Cambridge on June 3. Greene at once set about molding
the three regiments into what soon were recognized as the
best disciplined and best equipped units of all the raw
troops sent by the colonies to the aid of the beleaguered
town of Boston. Greene had Varnum as colonel of one
regiment, and his brother Christopher was a major with
Varnum. Samuel Ward, Junior, another close friend, was a
volunteer officer.

The Americans, scarcely more than a "rabble in arms,"
threw up breastworks on Breed's Hill about the middle of
June, while Greene was home briefly, winding up his
affairs in anticipation of a long, hard-fought war. The British took Breed's Hill and nearby Bunker Hill on June 17 at
a heavy toll in lives on both sides. Despite their defeat,
the Americans were encouraged by the fact that they
stood up so well against British regulars.

When George Washington arrived in Cambridge on July 2 to take command of the Continental Army, Greene, with 200 picked men of his Rhode Island brigade, was chosen to act as a welcoming escort. At that first meeting Washington and Greene formed an almost instant personal and military friendship. Greene for years had admired and respected Washington from afar. He knew of his record in the French and Indian War and his open and defiant stand for liberty. Now Greene gave the new commander in chief profound respect, unquestioning loyalty, willing obedience, and unbounded faith.

Washington was ten years older and a keen judge of men. He saw at once that Nathanael Greene was bold, impulsive but disciplined, and always prepared for the worst. His frank, confiding, loyal nature was immediately apparent. Soon the commander in chief learned that Greene never was petty or mean. He made friends easily and kept them, and he was respected, even beloved by his officers and men, even though from the first he showed himself to be a strict disciplinarian.

Sometimes, when the stupidity or the timidity of others annoyed him, Greene could be abrupt, even ill-tempered. But usually he was patient and tactful in command. He had a high sense of personal honor and a respect for his superiors, but never cringed to any man. Washington could understand as well as like him, for such were his own outstanding attributes.

Washington quickly came to depend on Greene, for they thought much alike. Besides, the Rhode Island anchor smith's salty, homespun witticisms on life, men, and events were amusing to the fox-hunting aristocrat from Virginia. Perhaps, too, Washington had been favorably impressed by the almost perfect "spit and polish" of the 200-man detail of Rhode Island troops that had turned out under Greene's personal command to greet him. He had not expected quite as much from raw militia. Washington also early learned that Greene not only was the best strategist and tactician in the Army, he seemed to have a sense of foresight that told him what the enemy was most likely to do.

Officers never ceased to be fascinated by Greene's habit of seeming indifference when they were making a verbal report. He tilted back in his chair, folded his hands across his ample waistcoat, closed his eyes, and, to all appearances, soon was sound asleep. However, if there came a pause in the narration, or some obscure point was left unclear, the blue eyes opened wide and bored into the other man. When the report was ended, Greene nodded slowly and sometimes issued a low-toned, decisive order. But at other times he again closed his eyes, perhaps for minutes at a time, until he had reached a decision. Then he gave the order, in such clear terms that no one could fail to understand. While he seemed to be sleeping he had been sorting out the problem outlined by the report, breaking it down into separate parts, then putting it together again until he had what he felt was the right answer. He had been analyzing problems this way all his life, even when he had to work out a plan to make an anchor. And seldom was he wrong in his conclusion. Perhaps his deep study of mathematics helped.

Greene from the first insisted there should be a single Army command and that enlistments should run for the duration of the war. The Army must be truly Continental, representing all the colonies. Short militia enlistments were not enough, since a commander never would know how many men were available for a campaign. Greene early saw the interests of all the colonies as identical, and on October 19, 1775, he hinted in a letter that he favored independence. At that time even some members of Congress were against separation from Great Britain.

"The alternative is separation from Great Britain or subjugation to her," he wrote to Samuel Ward, Senior, who was in Philadelphia as a member of Congress. France, Greene said, was right in "refusing to intermeddle" until she was sure there would be "no hope of accommodations" between America and Britain to bring about peace.

He wrote to Ward in January, 1776: "Permit me to recommend a declaration of independence." Greene told Ward that America needed the navies of France and Spain to help on the sea and with military stores. This help could not be had until the colonies cut loose.

Greene, far better than Washington, understood the

temper and thinking of the common men and women of
the colonies, for he was closer to their everyday lives. He
was of great help to his chief in this respect, for Washington's temper frequently flared up when he learned of
the high prices charged by farmers and merchants for
supplies. "A good politician," Greene suggested, "must
and will consider the temper of the times and the prejudices of the people he has to deal with, when he takes his
measures to execute any great design." And, understanding men and their weaknesses, he knew how to anticipate
some of Washington's problems in a practical way. The
great leader himself thought all men who loved their
country should be as eager as he to work unselfishly for
the general good, instead of in their own interests.
Greene, the pragmatic Quaker, knew that most men were
not made of such heroic stuff.

The test of the soundness of Greene's military judgment
came rather soon. At a council of war in Washington's
headquarters in Cambridge, the advisability of mounting
an immediate attack on Boston was debated. Sir William
Howe, who had succeeded General Gage, had fortified
Breed's Hill and Bunker Hill after the Battle of Bunker
Hill, and he had thrown up strong entrenchments on
Boston Neck. The British held an impregnable position.
Greene's emphatic vote was "No," and he told the council
why. The Continental Army, with supposedly almost
17,000 men, lacked cannon, muskets, and powder for such a

risky venture, and the cost in lives would be heavy. The British, however, were securely shut up in Boston, Greene pointed out, and surely if slowly they were starving. They were sick from scurvy, because they could not get enough of the right kind of food or enough food at all. Fast, well-armed private ships of war were capturing most of the British supplies, and the British Navy seemed unable to keep the sea-lanes open. Time was on the side of the Americans, if Washington could keep his Army together and recruit enough men for the duration. Greene won his argument, for Washington agreed with him. The Army concentrated on drilling and procuring men and supplies.

While Greene was away in 1775, his first child was born in Coventry. The boy was named George Washington Greene, in honor of the commander in chief of the American Army.

Late in the autumn Martha Washington joined her husband in Cambridge. Greene then brought up Caty and the baby from Rhode Island. As a result there was gaiety at headquarters in the winter of 1775 and 1776, and Greene lived under somewhat more homelike conditions. Martha Washington and Caty Greene at once became as firm friends as their husbands already were, despite the difference in their ages.

Boston had been under siege since June, 1775, and something had to give soon. By New Year's Day, 1776,

Washington was becoming apprehensive. His new Continental Army had a paper strength of 8212, with only 5582 men fit for duty. But he had other plans for breaking the stalemate. He sent Greene's close friend, Major General Henry Knox, chief of artillery, to the already captured Fort Ticonderoga on Lake Champlain to haul overland in the dead of winter the most serviceable of the fort's cannon. Knox accomplished the stupendous job, barging down the lakes and sledging over snow-covered hills fifty-nine usable cannon. The biggest was a 24-pounder nicknamed Old Sow. On the night of March 2, under cover of a terrific American bombardment from emplacements surrounding the city, some twenty of the biggest of Knox's cannon were hauled by oxcart on sledges onto Dorchester Heights. They were mounted on the frozen earth, and defenses were built of logs and brush on the hard-packed snow. Next morning General Howe saw what the Americans had done and realized that he either must capture the guns by a costly frontal assault or evacuate Boston. The cannon placed both his army and British warships in Boston harbor in peril of destruction. Washington had accomplished something that Howe had thought could not be done.

A violent rainstorm prevented Howe from trying to break out of the American encirclement to take Dorchester Heights. When the storm ended it was too late. All of the American cannon had been hauled to the Heights and emplaced, and the earthworks had been greatly strengthened.

Reluctantly Howe evacuated Boston on March 17, 1776, and sailed away with the British fleet. Washington ordered Nathanael Greene to take command in the city.

# 4

## Victory from Disaster
★★★★★★★★★★★★★★

Two weeks later, sure that Howe would join other British forces to capture New York, either then or later, Washington sent Greene's brigade overland to New London, Connecticut, and from there Commodore Esek Hopkins, an old Rhode Island friend of Greene's ferried the troops up Long Island Sound to Brooklyn. There Greene completed the strong earthworks that General Charles Lee, then Washington's second in command, already had started. Lee was a former British officer of long experience, which perhaps was why Washington had appointed him to second place. But already Lee was jealous of Greene and Knox and other officers who were close to the commander in chief.

While watching a detachment of artillery drilling, Greene met young Captain Alexander Hamilton, a West Indian, and was so impressed by the young man's appearance and ability that he introduced him to Washington at the first opportunity. Soon Hamilton was on Washington's staff.

Combined British forces under the overall command of Howe, aided by Sir Henry Clinton and Earl Charles Cornwallis, newly arrived from the South, easily captured Long Island, including Brooklyn Heights, key to the defenses, in a wide encircling movement on August 27. Greene was ill in bed with a high fever on the day of the battle, so General Israel Putnam of Connecticut and General John Sullivan, a Maine native, led the defenders. In one of the most masterly retreats in history, Washington, with the help of a corps of Marblehead, Massachusetts, fishermen, secretly managed to ferry the Long Island half of his army over the narrow East River onto Manhattan Island, which Congress had ordered him to hold.

Greene, promoted on August 1 to major general, got up from a sick bed on September 7 to attend a council of war at headquarters in New York. The American Army, he told his brother officers, should not attempt to defend New York, as Congress insisted. Two thirds of the 25,000 inhabitants were Tories anyway, and they owned most of the property, which Greene insisted should be burned when the Americans retreated. If Washington remained on Manhattan Island, the British, with control of the sea approaches, could land troops behind him, cut him off, and force him to surrender. That development would end the Revolution.

Two small earthwork forts—Washington on Harlem Heights and Lee on the Palisades across the Hudson River in New Jersey—already had been constructed at Greene's urging. The Americans could retreat and make a stand in Harlem, he insisted, retreat to Fort Washington if they had to, and then, if it could not be successfully defended, escape across the Hudson to Fort Lee. But remaining on Manhattan Island, which could not be defended against both an army and a fleet, would be military suicide. Greene left the meeting "with a heavy heart" when the council voted to defend Manhattan.

Four days later, on September 2, a group of officers presented a petition to Washington, asking that New York be abandoned. They had come around to Greene's way of thinking. But precious time had been lost. Howe suddenly attacked, and Washington only narrowly escaped annihilation or capture of his entire force. At Harlem Heights Greene first came under fire. He had volunteered, with other officers, to go into the midst of the battle to encourage the troops. His own men were not engaged.

After a battle at nearby White Plains, Washington crossed the Hudson, leaving Greene in overall command of both Forts Washington and Lee. Greene took his post at Fort Lee. Fort Washington fell, under a strong British attack, and Washington took full responsibility since he had not ordered evacuation of the fort in time.

General Charles Lee hoped that if, for this serious error, Washington were removed from command by Congress, he himself would win the coveted post of commander in chief. He at once began a vitriolic attack on both Washington and Greene. It came to nothing, but Lee continued to give Washington a great deal of trouble. Greene, always suspicious of Lee's methods and judgment, never trusted the man again.

Greene may not have known so then, but already Washington had decided that "if he were killed or captured Greene was the best qualified of all his generals to succeed him as commander in chief," says Theodore Thayer, a recent Greene biographer. And Tench Tilghman, a member of Washington's staff described Greene as "a proper man" to take over.

Another side of Greene, recognized by both officers and men, was revealed in a letter he sent home: "People coming from home with all the tender feelings of devotion to domestic life are not sufficiently fortified with natural courage to stand the shocking scenes (of war) unless fortified with military pride." Thus Greene, while maintaining strict military discipline, could make allowances for human weaknesses.

Despite the debacle at Fort Washington, in which he

had overestimated the stamina of the American troops and the ability of some of their officers, Greene could write: "Our soldiers are as good as ever were; and were officers half as good as the men, they would beat any army on the globe of equal numbers." He blamed the "conduct of the officers," not the failure of the common soldiers, for the defeats the Continental Army suffered in 1776, especially on Long Island and at Fort Washington.

Washington left Greene in command at Fort Lee, on the Jersey Palisades, while he marched south and west. Charles Lee, in complete disregard of Washington's orders, delayed crossing the Hudson, then, when he did cross, went off on his own private campaign, which was no campaign at all. Vainly did Washington try to coax the recalcitrant and jealous Lee to join him with a big part of the divided army. Lee still went his own way.

Meanwhile, Greene set up supply depots for 20,000 men for three months through the Jerseys, on the road to Philadelphia. Already, on his own initiative, he was acting as a quartermaster general while still commanding the rear guard.

Then on the night of November 19 and 20 Lord Cornwallis himself belatedly crossed the Hudson. He expected to catch Greene napping at Fort Lee and bag his entire force. Then he would capture Lee, and finally Washington. The plan seemed easy enough to his Lordship and to

Sir William Howe. But an alert American mounted patrol had been sent out by the ever-watchful Greene to guard against just such a surprise move. The cavalrymen galloped back to the Fort, giving the alarm. Even so, Greene barely managed to pull out his force ahead of Cornwallis, and he had to abandon thirty badly needed cannon and most of his supplies.

A grim game of hare and hounds across the New Jersey flatlands followed. It has been described by military tacticians as one of the most brilliant and important in history.

# 5

## Trenton and Princeton
★★★★★★★★★★★★★★

Washington, joined by Greene, crossed the winter-raging Delaware River near Trenton and bivouacked on the west side. Greene had seized every available boat on the river for seventy miles above Philadelphia. When Cornwallis drove in for what he expected would be a quick kill, he found himself checkmated at the riverbank. There was no way to get his army across the ice-caked flood. Sorely disappointed, his lordship pulled his Army back and went into winter quarters. But he was careful to leave strong detachments at Trenton, Princeton, and several nearby towns to pin Washington down beyond the river. Most of these troops were Hessian mercenaries, hired by George III from the Margrave of Hesse in Germany.

Despite the grinding ice cakes and bitter cold and sleet, Washington crossed the Delaware with men, horses, and guns on Christmas night, 1776, in a howling blizzard. With Greene commanding the crucial left wing of the army, and Major General John Sullivan on the right, Washington surprised the Hessians—groggy after a night of holiday revelry—in a dawn battle on December 26 on the sleepy streets of Trenton. Guns and badly needed ammunition comprised most of his booty, but more important for the ragged, cold, and hungry little army, and for the country, was the victory itself. It gave new courage to the soldiers, and it fired the will of patriots everywhere to continue the unequal struggle for independence.

In another foray across the Delaware, four days later, in which Greene and 300 picked men led the van, Washington was trapped by Cornwallis behind a small creek. His back was to the ocean at his right rear and to the Delaware River at his left. "We shall bag the old fox in the morning," gleefully exclaimed Cornwallis, content to wait until daybreak to attack again. But during the night Washington crossed the creek and made a surprise move around the British left flank. He was careful to leave a rear guard to stoke the campfires, thus deceiving the enemy. Marching north, he defeated another British force at Princeton, and then, before Cornwallis could catch up, he retreated to the safety of Morristown in the highlands of New Jersey. There he went into winter quarters. From this haven he could watch the British and keep ready to counter any move they might make.

Cornwallis couldn't safely attack Washington in his carefully chosen stronghold in the hills, and his own flank was exposed by the American maneuver, so the British commander withdrew to a safer distance. Howe, whose army thus was immobilized, recalled Cornwallis to New York and abandoned New Jersey to the Americans. But Howe spent all that winter planning a spring attack on the American capital in Philadelphia, where independence had been proclaimed on the previous July 4.

Washington and Greene were in almost daily contact at this time. When, in December, leaders in Rhode Island sent an urgent message requesting that Greene be detached and sent home to help defend the state against the British, who had seized Newport, Washington firmly refused. He needed the Rhode Island general at the Morristown headquarters.

During the spring of 1777, with a British army under Gentleman Johnny Burgoyne poised for an attack from Canada through the lakes and the Hudson River valley, Greene and Knox were sent to pick the site of a fort to control the river. They chose West Point, New York. During the winter Washington had tried to persuade Congress to promote Greene to the rank of lieutenant general, but failed. Congress was wary of any rank higher than that of major general for anyone except Washington.

Greene wasn't too keen on the promotion anyway. If it had come through, he might have been assigned permanently to staff work, and he liked the excitement and the responsibilities of a line officer's post.

At the same time there was important personal news for Greene. On March 11, 1777, Caty's second child, a daughter, was born in Coventry. Long before the happy event, the Greenes had decided that if the baby proved to be a girl, she should be named Martha Washington Greene, in honor of Caty's close friend.

This period was a time of reorganization and planning at Morristown. Greene felt strongly that far too many incompetent army officers had been sent over to North America. Most of them had been hired by Silas Deane, one of the American commissioners to France. Greene was highly suspicious of a number of them, and in each such instance his hunch proved right. Exceptions included the young French Marquis de Lafayette; Baron Friedrich Wilhelm von Steuben; François L. de Fleury; Charles Armand, a French marquis and a dashing cavalryman; Thaddeus Kosciusko, a Polish engineer; Count Casimir Pulaski of Poland; and Lord William Alexander Stirling, a Scots officer and one of Washington's abler generals. These highly efficient men and patriotic officers became Greene's lifelong friends.

But when Deane, aided by Congress, tried to replace able American officers with flamboyant misfits, Greene was bitingly outspoken. Washington, although sharing his opinion, usually preferred to have Greene lead the fight rather than to inject himself openly into the row. And Greene never hesitated to do battle for a friend, no matter what the personal consequences to himself.

Then Deane made the supreme mistake of sending over one Philip C.T. du Coudray, a jobless French officer. Congress was persuaded to make du Coudray chief of artillery in place of the able and loyal Major General Henry Knox. A little inquiry showed Greene that du Coudray was far less able than he had been represented. Besides, Knox was doing a good job. Greene, Knox, and Sullivan at once threatened to resign their commissions if du Coudray got the post. Greene was courteous but unrestrained in his controversy with Congress. Indeed, he was so scathing that even John Adams, who rated him highly, told him plainly that he should either resign or apologize. Greene did neither, but the best that du Coudray could get after that argument was the rank and pay of a major general, with the innocuous title of inspector general. The man was drowned sometime later in the Schuylkill River, but Greene had won his point all the way. He had saved the morale of the whole officer corps, if not the Army itself.

Fort Ticonderoga, key to Lake Champlain, fell to the British on June 6, 1777. Major General Philip Schuyler, then in command of the Northern Army, sent a hurried call for Greene to come and help him stop Gentleman Johnny Burgoyne, who was marching down from Canada to New York in an attempt to capture the Hudson River and lakes George and Champlain. Washington refused to part with Greene, sending Benjamin Lincoln and Benedict Arnold instead. Greene was too badly needed in New Jersey, because Howe's intention to descend upon Philadelphia had become apparent.

General Horatio Gates, an ex-British officer who had settled in Virginia, managed to convince Congress that the aristocratic, wealthy, and able Schuyler was responsible for the fall of Ticonderoga. Thus, Gates got the command of the Northern Army for himself. Schuyler later was exonerated by a court-martial, but, for the time being, Gates was the man who would oppose Burgoyne and save the line of the Hudson, if he could. Washington gave Gates as many men as he could spare, stripping his own army to the bone to do so, but he had troubles of his own shaping up.

By a clever bit of maneuvering, Washington led his own forces back to the vicinity of Trenton while Howe and Cornwallis were convoying an army by sea around the Delaware Capes, up the Chesapeake to the Head of Elk, south of Wilmington, Delaware. Their objective quite clearly was Philadelphia, from which Congress had fled. The shorter Delaware River route was blocked by a chain of American forts.

Burgoyne was close to a showdown with Gates and his American army at Saratoga. The British already held Newport, Rhode Island, threatening all of New England, because Narragansett Bay, deep enough for the heaviest British warships, penetrated Rhode Island northward for twenty miles from the sea. And, if he chose, command of the sealanes would enable Howe to make another thrust toward one or more of the Southern ports. But, for the moment, Philadelphia was his objective.

# 6

## Brandywine
★★★★★★★★★★★★★

On August 25 Washington and a small group of officers, including Nathanael Greene and the newly arrived Marquis de Lafayette, watched the debarkation of Howe's troops at the tip of Chesapeake Bay. The Rhode Islander and the French aristocrat were meeting for the first time. Going on this scouting trip was a foolhardy venture. All, including Washington, might have been captured, as he later admitted. The group spent the night at the farm home of a patriot, then rode back to the main American army.

Although Howe and Cornwallis had debarked on August 25, Howe as usual was dilatory and waited to give battle until September 19. Washington had chosen Red

Clay Creek, south of Philadelphia, as the spot at which to dispute the British advance. Most of his officers agreed that he must block Howe at once or the British could push on unopposed to Philadelphia.

"General Howe," Greene tartly retorted in the war council, "will not think of such a thing until he has beaten this army. And you cannot hold your ground at Red Clay Creek!"

Greene had his way, and Washington instead decided to make his stand at Chadds Ford, on the east bank of Brandywine Creek, a branch of the Delaware River. There, as Greene pointed out, he would have the advantage of higher ground than the enemy's. After all, Washington had only 11,000 men to Howe's 15,000. Again, fortunately, the commander in chief decided to take the advice of his most able tactician.

Greene was given command of the left center, with Sullivan on the right. In Greene's division was Colonel George Weedon with his stalwart Virginia regiment.

Howe, unknown to Washington, had decided on a wide encircling movement of the American army. The maneuver was the same simple one in reverse that had worked so successfully for the British at the Battle of Long Island. Howe sent General Baron Wilhelm von Knyphausen, commanding his right, to make a strong feint at Washington's strongest segment. Then he swung, with Corwallis and the main army, around to the left, to get behind the Americans and roll up their flank.

And because both Washington and Sullivan had failed to reconnoiter the upper fords of the Brandywine, Howe's trick succeeded. Before Washington, who rode with Greene on the left center, knew what was happening the British were forcing Sullivan backward. Heavy cannonading and musketry fire rather than accurate intelligence gave the alarm. The commander in chief sent Greene and his division, which included the ex-innkeeper Weedon's regiment and the ex-pastor Brigadier General Peter Mühlenberg's regiment, at the double quick through the late September afternoon to the rescue of Sullivan. They would try to bolster the panicked troops. The reinforcement was too late, Greene suspected, to save the battle, but his men might keep the army intact if they could reach Sullivan in time.

Sullivan's force had broken under the unexpected British attack and rapidly was becoming disorganized when Greene's sprinting troops came up. There was no time now to try to stop Sullivan's fleeing men. Greene's soldiers fixed bayonets and plunged into the charging British line. Smoke and the thickening haze of late afternoon in the river valley made the distinction between friend and foe difficult as Greene's men, on order, opened their ranks, allowing Sullivan's men to pass quickly through to the rear. Then the American ranks closed, and a relentless barrier of steel and musket fire halted the British charge.

The battle swayed back and forth as the sun slowly sank. Cornwallis, watching from nearby, wished that he

could have just one more hour of daylight. Time after
time the enemy's cold steel pressed forward, but the
American line under Greene held compact and firm, pour-
ing a steady fire into the ranks of Grenadiers, Hessians,
Ansbachers, and light infantry. Soon Greene's enfilading
artillery under Knox began to take a heavy toll, causing
the enemy's lines to quiver and bend like a cornfield in a
whirlwind.

Cornwallis, still watching, shouted, "To the bayonet!
To the bayonet!"

Broken British ranks re-formed for a new attack, as the
Grenadiers smiled grimly under their black caps. The
mustachioed Hessians rushed to the charge.

Suddenly through the swirling smoke and mist the
soldierly form of Brigadier General Peter Gabriel Mühlenberg, organizer of the Eighth Virginia regiment of
Germans and one of Greene's ablest commanders, towered
above the charging infantrymen. He rode like a centaur.

The ground between the two lines was strewn with the
dead and dying as Mühlenberg's dark eyes swept the field
with an appraising glance, as steady as though he were on
parade. To the Hessians the sight of this giant man on a
powerful white horse meant nothing except another tar-
get. But he sent a shiver of cold fear along the line of the
Ansbachers. Old soldiers among them recognized in Mühlenberg the man who, only a decade before while studying in Germany for the Lutheran ministry and acting on a

wild, boyish prank, had served in their ranks for a time in a Göttengen regiment. He had left with them the impression of an inflexible will and an impetuous temper. The stern preacher of prewar days had not changed much, and his sudden appearance produced a frightened cry from the German ranks, *"Hier kommt Teufel Piet!* (Here comes Devil Pete!)"

The Ansbachers knew that where Devil Pete led there was need for all the strength and courage they could muster, and they braced themselves for the shock. That strength was required, indeed, for the battle became one of bayonet against bayonet, cold steel against cold steel. Thrust for thrust, men matched their strong arms, skill, wits, and trickery against each other. Charge followed charge as the sun sank slowly behind the trees.

Brigadier General Anthony Wayne, driven in on the left by Knyphausen, long since had re-formed his brigade behind Greene's division and was helping valiantly to repulse the British attempt to break through.

Then the gallant Weedon, overborne at last by sheer weight of numbers, was forced to draw off behind Mühlenberg's rear. Greene, driven back to a narrow pass on the Chester road, slowly began to draw off his men, who fired in deliberate volleys as they retired. He had accomplished his mission and given the broken divisions time to retreat in good order. Twilight deepened and darkness drew a swift curtain across the battlefield. Cornwallis broke off the action. Then slowly Greene led his exhausted men back toward their camp in Chester. His calm intervention and masterly rear guard action had saved the army. The battle was a defeat and a bad one, but Washington's men would live to fight another day.

After Brandywine, Greene was displeased because Washington failed to cite Colonel Weedon's regiment for its gallantry in helping to save Sullivan's men and in protecting the retreat of the main army. Greene apparently wasn't particular about himself, but thought Weedon should have been given some credit. Washington's explanation was simple and direct. "Everyone says you are my favorite general," he reminded Greene. Weedon had been serving under Greene and, like Washington, was a Virginian. If the commander in chief cited Weedon above others, he might be accused of partiality, and this suspicion would not be good for morale. The reply satisfied Greene.

# 7

## Germantown
★★★★★★★★★★★★★★

For more than three weeks after the battle of the Brandywine the armies of Washington and Howe maneuvered in
Pennsylvania, each trying to catch the other napping and
strike a mortal blow.

On September 26 Cornwallis occupied half-deserted
Philadelphia, from which most all of the inhabitants but
Tories had fled. Still, Howe had to destroy the American
Army to insure his own safety. His brother, Admiral Lord
Richard Howe, had been given the task of destroying the
small, weak American forts on the Delaware River, which
had forced General Howe to use the longer Chesapeake
Bay route to Philadelphia.

From the North came the cheering word that Gates, with the help of Arnold, Lincoln, and Fighting Dan Morgan and his Virginia riflemen, had beaten Burgoyne in a battle at Stillwater, near Saratoga, two days after the battle of the Brandywine. But Gentleman Johnny had entrenched his forces a mile away and still posed a serious threat to the control of the Hudson River, especially if Clinton should send troops northward from New York in time to help him.

Down in Pennsylvania, Washington was watching his chance. Howe's main army lay sprawled in a big camp, without entrenchments, at Germantown, five miles northeast of Philadelphia, following the occupation of the city by Cornwallis. On the morning of October 4 Washington struck at Howe in a carefully planned but complicated surprise attack. He sent Greene in command of the left and Sullivan the right in two flanking columns. Each had the job of rolling up the British from his side. Washington, keenly aware that Sullivan was under heavy criticism in Congress because of the defeat at Brandywine, rode with Sullivan himself, ready to take personal command if necessary.

Greene had two miles farther than the others to march, and, because of heavy fog that settled over the area, his guide lost the way. Thus Sullivan engaged the enemy three quarters of an hour before Greene's left wing could come into action. This delay threw the burden of the initial engagement on Sullivan's division and Wayne's brigade. By the time Greene reached the scene the battlefield was in great confusion. Shortly afterward, in the fog and smoke, Wayne's men became entangled with the brigade of General Adam Stephen, sent forward by Greene to their aid. Sullivan's and Wayne's men, their ammunition nearly gone, thought they were surrounded, broke, and ran.

Meanwhile, the British had rallied their forces around the strongly built Chew House in the center of Germantown. Artillery failed to knock out the building, and the battle for some time swirled around this temporary fort.

With Sullivan's and Wayne's lines broken and retreating in panic, and Mühlenberg's eager Virginians so far ahead of the line that most of them were taken prisoner by the British in Howe's overrun camp, Greene suddenly found himself the pivot on which the safety of the entire army depended. The British had taken refuge inside stone dwellings, encircled by high garden walls, which made excellent breastworks. Even Knox's cannon were of little use. Smoke from gunpowder and burning hay, mixed with thick fog, limited the visibility to forty yards. Distinguishing friend from foe was difficult.

Greene found himself between two fires as Howe wheeled his line and Cornwallis came up with fresh troops from Philadelphia. Washington, Sullivan, Wayne, and their officers rallied the panicked troops, restoring some semblance of order, while Greene threw his men in front of the again advancing British.

Greene's officers watched anxiously as he recklessly exposed himself amid the thick hail of musket balls. But he knew where men looked for encouragement in danger. A firm brow and a confident countenance were better sometimes than ammunition. Greene in his blue uniform with buff facings seemed to be everywhere, utterly disregarding the danger.

There came a renewal of enemy musket fire. Seemingly it intensified as Cornwallis with his fresh troops tried to end the struggle quickly. If he were to beat the Americans, then was the time to do so. Experience had shown him that tomorrow might be too late.

Queues and curls were the headdress for officers in that day, and both Greene and his aide, Captain Robert Burnet, each wore a queue, a little pigtail that hung at the back of the neck from a wig. "Burnet," observed the general with a little smile, as they strove to keep their reformed line intact, "you had better jump down, if you have the time, and pick up your queue."

The young aide grinned. "And your curl, too, General," he said, for a musket ball at that very moment had snipped off one of the curls on Greene's powdered white wig. The general smiled broadly at the jest, and men nearby, hearing the exchange, were heartened, and passed the joke along to others in the ranks. Surely, if General

Greene could joke with an aide about such a trifling matter as a wig and a curl in the thick of battle, things couldn't possibly be as bad as they seemed. The renewal of confidence was contagious, and the men loaded and fired their muskets with calm deliberation and careful aim in the thickening mist and rolling smoke.

The American cannon were making even more smoke than the British guns as Knox's cannoneers had time to load and fire their fieldpieces behind the American lines holding firm with musketry fire. Every effort Cornwallis made to break the solid defense line Greene had formed split on the stubborn resistance of the Rhode Islander's inspired men. They fought like demons with ever greater confidence. Their line had held under Greene at Brandywine against the cream of the British and Hessian armies. Surely they could hold it again—and they did. Even the precious American cannon were saved, including a dismounted gun that Greene ordered onto a farm wagon, to be trundled off to the rear.

For five miles the men slowly retreated under the heaviest fire the British could concentrate on Greene's exhausted division, while the main army fell back. Then came a lull in the fighting. Cornwallis, realizing that he could not break Greene's retreating line, had called a halt. His men had taken a terrible beating from Knox's cannon and the deliberate marksmanship of Greene's men.

Indeed, Cornwallis had broken off the action permanently. He did not intend to pursue Greene. There still was a weary march of fifteen miles back to the American bivouac, but Greene's men were almost happy despite their wounds and their fatigue. Although they had been beaten, largely because Sullivan's and Wayne's men had panicked, they had demonstrated real courage. True, the battle was another defeat, but in a way it had been a kind of victory. It had shown, due to the steadfastness of the Quaker general, that disciplined American troops, properly and bravely led, could stand up against the best the British Army could send against them.

The second battle of Saratoga was fought three days later, on October 7, 1777. Burgoyne, in one last gamble, shattered his badly crippled army against the Americans in their fortified position on Bemis Heights. He was forced out of his own entrenchments and hastily retreated with heavy losses. With no hope of getting help from Clinton in New York, low on food and ammunition, and with no safe line of retreat to Canada, Burgoyne was forced to surrender on October 17. The ambitious British campaign to crack the American defense line of the Hudson River had failed.

Washington, meanwhile, continued to watch Howe and Cornwallis in Pennsylvania until both armies went into winter encampment, the British in Philadelphia and the Americans at Valley Forge some twenty miles away. Washington picked a spot on the Schuylkill River that was

strongly defensible and from which he could pose a constant threat to Philadelphia while reorganizing his army
and waiting for the enemy's next move in the spring.

# 8

## Quartermaster General

★ ★ ★ ★ ★ ★ ★ ★ ★ ★ ★ ★ ★ ★

During the terrible winter months of 1777 and 1778 in the camp at Valley Forge, Nathanael Greene first began his work for Washington as quartermaster general. He operated without the rank, but with full authority.

And Greene showed how tough he was beneath his jovial exterior and amiable manner. The ragged, starving army, with bleeding, shoeless feet, needed everything— food, clothing, shoes, all kinds of supplies. Greene had one short, simply worded order from Washington: "Forage the country naked. Take all their cattle, sheep, and horses for the use of the Army." Both Washington and Greene had reached the end of their long patience with Americans who would not feed their soldiers, men who were

selling meat and provisions to the enemy in Philad(
for hard British gold.

"Two men were taken up carrying provisions t(
enemy yesterday morning," Greene reported one da
his chief. "I gave them a hundred (lashes) each by wa
example." Then he confiscated the provisions.

Greene began the establishment of a commissary
that ultimately would reach into all the colonies, and
set up secret and well-guarded Army depots from Che
peake Bay to upper New York State along the line of t
Hudson River. Brigadier General Thomas Mifflin, w.
still held the rank of quartermaster general, had not be(
with Washington's Army since it began to operate i
Pennsylvania. This sadly inefficient officer had been se
cretly engaged in a conspiracy to discredit Washington
General Gates and a recently appointed foreign office(
named Thomas Conway, another misfit, tried to persuade
Congress to shelve Washington and give to Gates, "the
hero of Saratoga," the commanding generalship. Greene,
at whom the so-called Conway Cabal also was aimed
since he was Washington's close friend and right-hand
man, described Conway as "a man of much intrigue and
little judgment." Conway, Greene acidly said, had been
"palmed off on the public" as a good military man. When
Conway received his promotion, Greene protested to
Congress, but to no avail. Conway held his commission
and continued to make trouble.

Ultimately Washington exposed Conway to Congress and, through him, Gates, Mifflin, and the others in the conspiracy. The plotters had misjudged the temper of the public and the fierce loyalty to Washington of members of the officer corps, led by Greene, Lafayette, and Alexander Hamilton. The conspirators quickly backed down when their plot was brought into the open and ran to cover. Gates penned a cringing letter of apology to his chief. Mifflin and Conway were shelved, but Gates had influence enough in Congress to get another chance.

But that winter was not all grim despair at Valley Forge. Most important to Greene personally was the fact that in January his beloved Caty joined him, and quickly the little log hut she shared with him became a kind of home. It also was the center of small social gatherings in the long, cold, snow-swept evenings. Martha Washington, Mrs. Knox, Lady Stirling, and the wives of other officers were in camp. The foreign officers especially were intrigued by Caty's charm, graciousness, and quick wit. Peter Duponceau, an impressionable young French aide to Baron von Steuben, wrote of her as a "handsome, elegant, and accomplished woman."

Never was Nathanael Greene's ability to master a very complicated subject more useful to him than when he took over the post of quartermaster general on February 25, 1778. He accepted the job reluctantly, at the insist-

ence of Washington, backed by Robert Morris, the financier and Congressman, and others in Congress, who promised him a free hand.

Greene insisted, however, that he retain his permanent rank of major general, for his first love was combat duty. He would have preferred taking only his major general's pay, but Congress pressed on him a one percent commission, to be split with his two chief assistants. He picked men he could trust for these posts, and he made his brother Jacob Greene, in Coventry, a commissary agent for Rhode Island.

More than anything save food, the troops needed horses and wagons for the transport of guns and supplies. By June 1, within three months, thanks to tireless days and sleepless nights, Greene had reorganized the Quartermaster Department and had it working at top efficiency. He was ready to move and feed the army anywhere Washington might send it.

Long before Washington left winter quarters in Valley Forge that spring, the British made it apparent that they would evacuate Philadelphia. After the two battles of Saratoga the previous fall, the enemy's only holdings were in Philadelphia, New York, and Newport. Howe went home in retirement aboard the seventy-four gun HMS *Andromeda*. Sir Henry Clinton took over command in North America.

When on June 17, 1778, the American Army's council of

war debated tactics, Washington, Greene, and some of the
other officers strongly favored attacking Clinton during
his march northward from Philadelphia to take ship to
New York. Greene was convinced that Clinton intended
to go there and that he would march part of the way.
General Lee, who had returned to duty after having been
taken a prisoner of war in 1776, just as strongly insisted
there should be no attempt to stop Clinton. The British
commander, Lee said, should be permitted to retreat to
New York unhindered. The council was undecided,
thanks to Lee.

Greene was deeply disturbed that Lee had managed to
cause a delay, perhaps giving the British time to escape
what easily could have been an American trap. He did not
give up, however, and quietly began to round up senti-
ment among other members of the staff, biding his time.

Seven days later, on June 24, Greene and Hamilton,
who was Washington's trusted aide, called on Washington
at his headquarters. Tradition says that Washington's
greeting was, "I know what you have come for. You want
me to fight." They did, and he agreed.

The opportunity was, indeed, too good to be passed up.
Clinton had intended to embark his troops near New
Brunswick, New Jersey. Washington, meanwhile, had
turned his flank and forced him to head for Sandy Hook as
an alternate embarkation point. The Americans caught up
with Clinton's twelve-mile-long column of Redcoats,
struggling in the heat and dust of the Jersey coastal plain on

June 28. Greene, acting in his dual capacity as a line officer and as quartermaster general, commanded the right of
the American front; Lee commanded the left. With no
other choice Clinton turned and formed his troops to defend his line of retreat.

Washington's plan was for Lee to initiate the action and
roll up the British right. Then Greene would lead with a
hard right punch at the enemy's left. But Lee, when the
time came to strike, mysteriously refused to give the
order. The uncertainty confused his men, and they
quickly broke ranks. Soon they were in disordered retreat,
with Lee making no effort to stop them.

Greene, bringing up his artillery to enfilade the enemy,
his men stubbornly holding their ground, again saved the
army in a moment of crisis. Washington spurred up front,
angrily removed Lee from command, then rallied the retreating left flankers. Lee later was court-martialed and
dismissed in disgrace. Some eighty years after both Washington's and Greene's suspicions would be proved true, for
Lee was a traitor rather than a coward, and he had been a
traitor for some time. A letter was discovered in a London
trunk written by Lee while he was a prisoner of war. In it
Lee had outlined a plan to defeat the Americans to Admiral Lord Howe and to Sir William Howe. The Howe
brothers did adopt a part of Lee's plan, but when it failed
they had kept it a deep secret, most likely not wanting the
world to know they had dealt with a traitor.

But all Washington knew at the end of June 28 was that

what had promised to be an excellent chance to bag Clinton's entire field army had been lost by the deliberate insubordination of Lee. He had Greene to thank once again for saving the army from a complete rout, but Clinton escaped by sea from Sandy Hook during the night.

The campaign next took an entirely different direction. News that France had become an open ally of the young United States had been received in the American Army camp in May. Soon Washington learned that Admiral Jean Baptiste Charles Henri, Count d'Estaing, with a French fleet and 4000 French troops was off the New England coast. For the first time the Americans would have the help of sea power.

The British were too strong for an American attack on New York, so Washington decided to hit them in Newport, with the help of the French. Sullivan was in command now in Rhode Island, and Greene, still retaining his rank of general of division, graciously consented to command a division under Sullivan, however much he privately may have doubted the wisdom of leaving his compatriot in command of the expedition. Sullivan was courageous, able, fiercely loyal to Washington, and a good friend to Greene, but he was impetuous. Sometimes his judgment did not match his bravery. There is evidence nonetheless that Washington rated him second only to Greene in military ability and leadership.

Admiral d'Estaing, sometime after the Americans had laid siege to Newport, became impatient at the delay in attacking and sailed out of Narragansett Bay to engage Admiral Howe's fleet. A two-day howling gale mauled both the French and the British fleets, and d'Estaing, badly crippled, decided to sail north to Boston to refit. The result was that Sullivan's assault in August, 1778, on the British lines before Newport, without the aid of the French Navy, failed. He had to retreat to the mainland by way of Tiverton.

Greene, in the midst of Sullivan's retreat, was eating breakfast at his headquarters on Tiverton Heights, across the narrow Sakonnet River. His hostess, a Quaker woman, burst into the room at the height of the cannonading. The sound of musket fire was approaching, and she urged the general to flee. "The British will have you, General!" she warned.

Greene paused, fork to mouth, smiled amiably and shook his head. "I will have my breakfast first, Madam," he replied. Then he tranquilly turned back to finish his hearty morning meal. He had been on his feet for forty-eight hours without rest, and he was hungry.

Caty Greene, high on the hills in the Greene home in Coventry, across Narragansett Bay on the west shore, could hear the roar of the guns and could see the smoke of battle. Only the deep little tidal river called the Sakonnet and the fast work of Brigadier General John Glover's

Marblehead boatmen enabled Sullivan, with the help of Greene, to get his troops safely onto the mainland. The day was perhaps a more anxious one for Caty than for her husband.

But one more task remained before Greene, after a brief stop at his Coventry home and in nearby East Greenwich, could return fully to his duties as quartermaster general. He was given the delicate assignment of smoothing over the ruffled feelings of Count d'Estaing. The impetuous Sullivan felt, and had said openly, that the French admiral had let the Americans down. In his attempt to keep harmony, Greene even went so far as to urge successfully that the Rhode Island legislature, sitting in East Greenwich, not permit Sullivan's critical letters to be read in open session. Good feeling between the French and American allies had to be maintained. As a result, d'Estaing wrote to Greene that while he was not personally insulted by Sullivan, he had felt that Sullivan's remarks might stir up bad feeling between the French and Americans.

# 9

## Treason
★★★★★★★★★★★★★

All during 1779 Washington and Greene anxiously and expectantly awaited the French help at sea that they needed to get the war off dead center. During this year the Greenes celebrated the birth of their third child, a girl, whom they named Cornelia Lott Greene, born in Coventry on September 23, 1779.

Finally a new French fleet arrived in Newport on July 10, 1780, with the promise of an even bigger armada to come, and the tactical situation changed overnight. Then Washington could plan a major attack. The stalemate that had been interrupted only briefly by local engagements could be broken. Admiral Chevalier d'Anzax de Ternay and General Count Jean Baptiste D. de Vimeur de Rochambeau, with 5000 French troops, would be under Washington's command. Admiral François J. P. de Grasse and an even more powerful fleet and army soon would sail from Brest.

But because of expected further British attempts to wrest from the Americans the control of the Hudson River, Washington suddenly moved part of his army nearer to West Point, key to the northern defense system. West Point already was stronger than Greene had envisioned it when he and Knox laid out the plans. Greene was left in New Jersey in command of the main army and the huge stores he had stockpiled as quartermaster general. Second in command, he was serving at this time in a dual capacity. Washington's move forced Clinton to postpone plans for an attack along the Hudson River.

When Washington departed on September 17 for a highly secret conference with Count de Rochambeau and Admiral de Ternay, he left Greene in command of the whole Army, with full authority to act in his absence. But Greene was under specific orders to march at once to Tappan, New Jersey, close by the Hudson. From there he could swing in any needed direction to meet a British threat. "I have such entire confidence in your prudence and abilities," Washington wrote, "that I leave the conduct of it to your discretion." Greene, nonetheless, was ordered not to "seek action, nor to accept one, but upon advantageous terms." Greene promptly instructed the men to "be in perfect readiness" and moved the troops to Tappan the next day.

So secret was Greene's move that he posted picked riflemen to stop any deserters on the march so that they could not carry news to the enemy. Greene's orders were to shoot to kill. By nightfall the men were in camp at Tappan.

The Hartford conference with the French leaders was productive of little more than good will, for the British, reinforced at sea, promptly had blocked de Ternay at Newport. Count de Rochambeau felt he had to keep his army with the fleet. Stalemate in the North seemed to have been resumed again for an indefinite period.

Major General Benedict Arnold, leader of a disastrous expedition to Quebec early in the war and a hero of Saratoga, where he lost a leg, recently had become commander at West Point by his own request. Despite his mercurial temper, Washington thought well of Arnold, whose courage had been tested on many battlefields. Neither Washington nor Greene, as temporary chief of the whole American Army, knew that as far back as May, 1779, Arnold had been in treasonous correspondence with Sir Henry Clinton. For a major generalcy in the British Army and $100,000 in gold, Arnold had agreed to hand over West Point to the British. For that purpose Arnold had wangled the command from the trusting Washington.

The plot was discovered on the morning of September

23 when Major John André, Clinton's favorite aide, was caught in civilian clothes while on his way back to board HMS *Vulture* in the Hudson River after making final secret arrangements with Arnold at West Point. André had landed below West Point in full uniform, but had been forced to change into civilian clothing to get through the American lines when the *Vulture* was fired upon by American batteries and had to drop down the river.

When Arnold, at breakfast in his West Point quarters, received word of the arrest of one John Anderson, the fictitious name André had used, he fled for his life to the *Vulture*. He forced his bargemen to row him down the Hudson at pistol point.

Greene learned of Arnold's treason at his headquarters in Tappan from Hamilton and hurried two regiments at forced march to West Point to reinforce the garrison. Then he alerted the entire Army, prepared to march at once if the British, despite the failure of Arnold's plot, showed any signs of attacking the key stronghold.

Washington, on his way back from the conference with de Rochambeau in Hartford, arrived in West Point just after Arnold's flight and André's arrest. He ordered André sent to Greene at Tappan. There, a few days later, Greene presided at André's court-martial. As president of the court, Greene broke a tie vote dooming André to be hanged as a spy. Nor could all the resulting pleas made by Clinton's emissaries change his mind.

When Colonel Beverly Robinson, Clinton's personal representative, brought a final note from Arnold himself, begging for André's life, Greene read it, then tossed the missive contemptuously at Robinson's feet.

"I will exchange André for Arnold," was Greene's acid comment, the usually genial countenance a mask and his blue eyes cold and hard. André was a brave man and a gallant officer, and Greene, like the others, realized that he was the victim of unfortunate circumstances, but this betrayal was a time to be tough-minded. Of course, Greene knew that Clinton could not agree to such a deal. André had to hang.

Greene paraded his entire army the next day to witness the hanging. Grimly he took André's formal salute as the officer, dressed in full uniform, walked with dignity and courage to the scaffold. The uniform was the one concession Greene would make.

For a long time Greene had sought release from his irksome duties as quartermaster general. He had reorganized the service and supplied the Army with most of what it needed, so far as this task could be done. He had been prudent in spending, and most of his agents had proved as honest as he hoped they would be. But Greene's unbroken record of success—as a combat officer, as quartermaster general, and as the closest adviser to Washington—had aroused the envy of many persons in the Army and in Congress. Greene once had said that any man who didn't expect to have enemies "was a fool." Then his enemies began to plague him, even to the extent of setting up a special board to supervise the Quartermaster Department. Congress would not listen to his plans for further improvement of the service. He was spending too much money, it was said, as Congressmen conveniently failed to recognize that their own shabby financing methods had caused Continental money to depreciate so fast that it had become almost worthless. Inevitably supplies for the Army cost more.

Finally, and with great reluctance, Washington accepted Greene's resignation as quartermaster general. He told Greene that he had given entire "satisfaction," with "strictest integrity." On September 30, 1780, Colonel Timothy Pickering was named to succeed Greene. But Pickering, who did a good job, also quickly found that this position was a difficult one.

Thus, a week after Arnold's treason, Greene found himself without assignment in the Army and asked for the command at West Point. There yet remained a big job to put the post in the best defensive condition. Washington gave Greene the command on October 6, but suggested that, contrary to Greene's hope for a quiet winter in garrison with his growing family, he might not remain there for long.

There was good reason for Washington's warning. General Gates, the hero of Saratoga in the autumn of 1777, had been sent south in June, 1780, when Brigadier General Benjamin Lincoln and 1600 men were captured by the British at Charleston, South Carolina. Lincoln had fought successfully for fifteen months in difficult terrain. He, too, had been one of the heroes of Saratoga, but in the South he had neither the men nor the equipment to make a longer fight. Gates, although exposed during the winter of 1777 and 1778 as one of the chief plotters in the Conway Cabal, had been sent in midsummer by Congress to command in the South. Washington was not consulted. Gates had able officers with him, including Baron Johann de Kalb and Marquis Charles Armand and his Partisan Legion, but he was not a man to listen to advice, particularly from men whom he regarded as inferior. He had the choice of taking one of two routes to the interior in pursuit of Lord Cornwallis, then in command in the South. One route led through good land, where he could expect support from patriotic farmers; the other led through desolate swamplands. He chose the swamplands as being more direct, and his army nearly starved on this hunger road. Finally Gates's tired and starving men met the British at Camden, South Carolina, on August 16, 1780, and they were badly beaten. With his decimated army Gates retreated to Hillsboro, North Carolina. Only because Cornwallis failed to follow up the victory with a hot pursuit did Gates manage to survive.

With Gates's shattering defeat went Washington's last

hope of holding the South. The Carolinas and Georgia were at the mercy of Cornwallis, and seemingly Virginia would be next. The British in their earlier efforts had failed to split the new states along the line of the Hudson River, but they were close to cutting them almost in half from the Atlantic Ocean to the Allegheny Mountains.

Even Congress realized that heroic steps had to be taken. Not only did it demand a court of inquiry for Gates, but, led by Southerners, there arose an instant and insistent demand that Nathanael Greene be sent to command in the South. Forgotten was the long and sometimes bitter quarrel between Greene and Congress. They wanted the man who was recognized as "second only to Washington," and nothing could have pleased Washington more. He named Greene to command the Southern department on October 14 and ordered him to leave at once.

Greene's appointment to command in the South "was a public declaration that the charges against his administration of the Quartermaster Department were false. Greene stood justified by the voice of the country," later wrote George Washington Greene, his grandson. And, except for the sniping of some historians since then—even up to the present day—that verdict also is history's.

"Your presence with your command as soon as possible is indispensable," was Washington's peremptory order to Greene. Thus, Greene did not have time for even a brief farewell with Caty, who was on the way to West Point from Rhode Island. They missed a hastily arranged rendezvous at Fishkill on the Hudson. Caty followed him as far as Philadelphia before finally returning home. For her to go farther South was much too dangerous.

# 10

## "As Dangerous As Washington"
★★★★★★★★★★★★★

When Lord Cornwallis learned that Greene was his new opponent, he repeated to his staff the comment he had made long before, "Greene is as dangerous as Washington; he is vigilant, enterprising, and full of resources. With but little hope of gaining an advantage over him, I never feel secure when encamped in his neighborhood."

Earl Charles Cornwallis, forty-two, a lieutenant general, was rated the best soldier England had sent to North America. He had fought Greene in all the campaigns in New York and New Jersey, and he thoroughly respected his ability. Accordingly, his lordship made plans for the toughest campaign of his career.

Greene reached Charlotte, North Carolina, on December 2, 1780. Even before Gates, with stiff politeness turned over the command to him, he had plunged into the task of reorganizing the ragged, half-starved army.

Gates had been as much Greene's enemy as Washington's during the Conway Cabal and long before, because he was a jealous man. The genial, smiling Rhode Islander, knowing this fact, nonetheless tried to make the changeover of command as easy as he could for the defeated older man. Gates never forgot the kindness, and ultimately he became Greene's friend.

South Carolina was completely in the hands of the enemy. Members of the legislature were in hiding in the swamps and in the hills. Governor John Rutledge had fled to North Carolina with a price on his head. The state was being torn apart even more by the civil war that then raged between Whigs and Tories than it had been by the invading British Army. Burning, pillaging, and wanton brutality were practiced by both sides. Hatred begot hatred. North Carolina was in little better condition. Georgia was ready to fall like a ripe plum into enemy hands. Only Virginia had escaped the worst ravages of the war.

Greene's new army, for the most part, was in rags. Some of the officers were almost destitute. Winter had set in. There were provisions for no more than three days for the 2307 soldiers, of whom only 909 were of the Continental

Line, men who had enlisted for the duration of the war. They were the hardened, trusted veterans. Food was procured on a hand-to-mouth basis by daily foraging in an area that already had been stripped nearly bare of provisions by both Americans and British. There were few horses and almost no wagons. Boards, nails, and horseshoes were primary needs.

Greene shared his first evening meal at Charlotte with his staff, eating the same food as the men in the ranks. Then he plunged into an all-night checkup to determine what he had on hand with which to fight Cornwallis. His aging commissary officer told fellow officers the next day that Greene, in one night, "understood the army's condition and the resources of the surrounding country better than Gates in the whole period of the campaign." But there were many long moments that first night in Charlotte during which Greene would rub his unshaven upper lip in reflective silence, a habit when he was thinking out a problem.

Within less than twenty-four hours after assuming command in the South, all the lonely, sleepless nights and the great abuse Greene had undergone as quartermaster general—a job he never had wanted—began to pay off. He knew from bitter experience just what he needed, what he had on hand, and how much and where to get the rest if it was to be had. And he knew, as he usually did, where to find the officers to help him feed and supply his army. He needed wagons, horses, food, hay and grain, and many other supplies, and quickly. These things he must wheedle or seize from patriots who already had been drained of nearly all their resources by the demands of battling armies for the past five years.

Lieutenant Colonel Edward Carrington, Virginia artilleryman, could do the job, and could be trusted. Greene had picked Carrington for quartermaster general even before reaching Charlotte. He sent for him and for young Lieutenant Colonel William R. Davie, twenty-four, of South Carolina. As the new head of the Commissary Department, Davie would know where to procure what was needed in the way of food and forage. Line and staff officer appointments could wait, but these men must be assigned at once if Greene were to keep together even this pitiably small army. "An army marches on its stomach," Napoleon Bonaparte would say much later, but none knew this fact better than Greene. He had worked out his plans on the long and tiring ride south on horseback.

Carrington, who had been with General Lincoln at Charleston, had a reputation as an able coordinator. His mind was fertile in expedients, and already Carrington's reputation for foresight and prompt, decisive, methodical action—some of Greene's own characteristics—was well-known.

Davie had lived in South Carolina since his parents had brought him over from England at the age of seven. Early in the war he had spent every shilling of his inheritance to raise and equip a troop of cavalry. Along with others, he had carried on a kind of private partisan war ever since the fall of Charleston. He was well educated and somewhat bookish, an interest that he shared with Greene. Sure of eye, sound of judgment, skilled in understanding of character, cool and self-possessed, he was just the man to run the Commissary Department. But the dashing life of a cavalryman was Davie's first love, and Greene, who always liked the life of the combat soldier far better than that of a quartermaster, understood how much Davie was sacrificing to serve where he was most needed.

The Carolinas and Georgia depended chiefly on rivers for transportation. There were few roads, and they were inferior. Many highways were impassable at certain times of the year. Great swamps lay between most of the streams—the Dan in North Carolina and Virginia; the Haw, the Cape Fear, the Yadkin, and the Catawba in North Carolina; the Pee Dee, the Congaree, Wateree, Santee, Saluda, Edisto, Ennore, and lesser streams in South Carolina; and the Savannah in Georgia. The vast swamps were fever ridden in the hot, sticky months. There were few areas of high ground until one got well inland. Except on the high savannahs where farming and grazing were carried on, the country was poor. Altogether this terrain was the most difficult along the entire Eastern seaboard in which to fight a war.

Greene, with his customary thoroughness, already had sent trusted officers to scout the rivers of North Carolina. He had decided while on the way south, and had so written to Washington, that since his army would be too weak for open combat, he would wage a kind of partisan warfare, seeking to harass the enemy rather than to attack him in the open. And since few wagons were likely to be available, he must depend upon the rivers for carrying supplies, guns, and sometimes men. But first he had sent these picked officers to sound the depth and measure the flow of the principal rivers in flood and in drought. The streams were known to be difficult to navigate, and in sudden rainstorms they often swelled within hours into raging torrents in which no small boat could live.

Greene had designed a boat "of a peculiar kind," which he intended to build in large numbers. These boats could carry forty to fifty barrels of goods, powder, and shot and "yet draw little more water than a common canoe half loaded." Army supplies could be moved swiftly and secretly in them while Cornwallis's troops still must plod laboriously over corduroy roads axle-deep in mire, his lordship's speed tied down to the slowest of his creaking supply wagons.

Since guerrilla war would be Greene's most important tactic, he must lean heavily upon two veterans of that dangerous hit-and-run game—Francis Marion and Thomas Sumter. Brigadier General Marion, the Swamp

Fox, was the will-o'-the-wisp scourge of the British Army in the South Carolina swamplands. This homely, emaciated, but tough and wiry descendant of French Huguenots, with a heavy price on his head, had been a wealthy upland planter and had fought in the Indian wars. But Marion's command seldom exceeded seventy men at any one time. They came and went as they pleased.

The taciturn Marion inspired fierce loyalty. He never had been surprised or defeated by the enemy. He was forever popping up in daring raids from his secret lair, Snow Island, which lay snugly deep in the swamps, safe from invasion. He was the type of leader on whom Greene counted the most. Marion's reputed vigilance, promptitude, activity, energy, dauntless courage, and his unshakable self-control were the qualities needed in a campaign against a numerically superior foe. Marion's fertile mind devised ways to seize from the British sizeable amounts of the enemy's supply of arms, ammunition, and other stores. But above all, what interested Nathanael Greene most was that men said the Swamp Fox was imbued with two principles—love of country and love of right—and that he was incorruptible.

Brigadier General Thomas Sumter, the Gamecock, was a man of very different kidney. The tall, hardy Sumter was dependable if he approved a superior's plan; otherwise he often went off on a tangent to suit his own ideas, sometimes upsetting battle plans. But Sumter had courage, he had the confidence of the patriots of South Carolina, and he was useful on limited assignments. After the fall of Charleston, Sumter's little band of ragged, ill-equipped partisans had kept the Tories down and had harassed the British in the watersheds and swamps of the Wateree, the Broad, the Ennore and Tiger rivers, so that Sumter was almost as famous as Marion.

No more able or courageous officer was available to Greene than General Daniel (Fighting Dan) Morgan, veteran of the French and Indian War and of most of the battles of the Revolution already fought in the North. The Old Wagoner, a Jersey man, had hot Welsh blood with a very low boiling point, but he was as kind as he was rough and stern. His men loved this tall, muscular, vigorous, clean-limbed man who had a clear, kindly eye and an open countenance. He was a man others liked at once, and none more so than Greene, whose friend he had been for years. Old Dan was only forty-five, despite his nickname, and he was good-humored, with a keen, rustic wit. He and Greene were alike in this respect, for Greene, too, had a salty tongue. At this time Morgan was troubled with increasingly painful attacks of rheumatism, the result of his many campaigns. Otherwise, he was as sound as a hazelnut. To Morgan and his Virginia riflemen, Gates had owed much of his success at Saratoga. Greene picked Morgan for second in command and sent for him at once.

Brigadier General Isaac Huger had fought in his native

South Carolina and in Georgia. This thirty-nine-year-old officer was recognized as thoroughly dependable. He had good sense, zeal, and intrepidity. He would be third in command.

Lighthorse Harry Lee, twenty-five, the dashing and impulsive Virginia cavalryman, and Lee's Legion of 280 horsemen and infantry had been especially assigned by Washington at Greene's urgent request. Lee was one of the few officers of the Revolution who was well educated. He was said to be the son of the lowland beauty whom Washington had loved years before he married Martha Custis. Lee had known Greene since Brandywine and had served under him at Germantown. They were close friends. Lee's Legion was the best mounted, best uni-formed, best armed unit in the Continental Army, and the horses were as well trained as the men. Lee was hurrying south by forced marches, but he could not be expected to arrive before the middle of January.

Colonel William Washington, twenty-eight, a distant Virginia relative of the commander in chief, was almost as well-known a cavalryman as Lee. Young Washington had been wounded at Trenton. Later he had served under Lincoln and Gates in the South. Not until after the defeat at Camden, however, had Gates, who had little use for cavalry, permitted Washington to recruit a larger troop of horses. But Greene fully appreciated the need for cavalry in scouting, screening infantry, and fighting rearguard actions during a retreat.

Washington, who rode as though he were a part of the horse, despite an inclination to stoutness, was springy of step, brisk in manner, and invariably good-humored. These qualities, too, were ones that Greene liked in an officer.

Just before Greene arrived to take command at Charlotte, young Washington once again had shown his mettle and the inventiveness that he always called into play when an unusual situation seemed about to thwart his plans. More than once his quick mind had enabled him to outsmart the enemy. At Rugeley's farm in South Carolina a detachment of well-trained Tories had dug in, using the farmhouse as a fort. The post was too well defended to make possible a direct charge against their heavy musket fire at close range. Only artillery could blast Rugeley and his Tories out. Nearby was a fallen log that, to Washington's eye, looked enough like a cannon to be the real thing. Quickly he had the log cut and shaped, mounted it on wheels from a farm wagon, and trundled it into position just near enough to the house for the Tories to see it. Convinced in the half-light of the dying day that it was, indeed, a cannon, they surrendered.

Thaddeus Kosciusko, the Polish general and colonel of engineers in the American Army since the start of the war, was thirty-five when he was assigned to Greene in the South. Kosciusko had served under Gates at Saratoga. He also had fortified West Point under the direction of Greene and Knox. Greene set Kosciusko to work immediately to choose a site for a new, stronger, and healthier camp. Within days Kosciusko reported favorably on a site at Cheraw Hills on the Pee Dee River. From there the army would have a better chance to compete with the British, who lay in camp at Winnsboro, seventy miles away.

Brigadier General Andrew Pickens, a South Carolinian, was courageous and cool headed, and he already had distinguished himself under Lincoln, in open field fighting as well as in guerrilla warfare.

Colonel Otho Williams had been well and favorably known to Greene during his long service in the North, and already they were warm friends. Greene's pleasure at having this gallant young officer available was indicated within minutes of his arrival at the Charlotte headquarters. Graceful of carriage, with a distinct military bearing, Williams had an open, expressive countenance that at once drew men to him and invited a trust that never was betrayed. He was warmhearted, expansive, but a stern disciplinarian, expecting and giving prompt obedience. His clear mind was valuable in war councils. He was ardent but prudent—two qualities Greene most admired in an officer, reflecting his own and Washington's approach to problems.

Now just thirty-one, Williams had been born in Maryland. At the outbreak of the war he had marched off eagerly to Boston and had served with distinction. He was a major when Fort Washington surrendered in the New York retreat and was taken prisoner. Exchanged, he had plunged again into the thick of the fighting. Williams had been deputy adjutant under Gates, but that pigheaded officer seldom listened to him. He almost never made use of Williams' wide knowledge of the South. The defeat at Camden might never have happened had Gates accepted Williams' urgent advice to take an alternate route that led through a friendly countryside.

# 11

## Greene's Big Gamble
★ ★ ★ ★ ★ ★ ★ ★ ★ ★ ★ ★ ★ ★

Almost at once Greene decided to divide his force, a bold step and, as he well knew, one that was in open violation of a fundamental principle of warfare. By this act he would take great risks, and, if defeated in battle, he would have no excuse to offer. But then Greene never believed in excuses anyway. Careful planning and a firm belief that "fortune favors the bold" were two cardinal rules of his military career.

Cornwallis was determined to seize North Carolina and Virginia. Indeed that aim was the principal reason the Rhode Islander had been sent to reorganize the shattered Southern army and attack the British before they could strike northward. But, following Gates's defeat at Camden, a band of Tories led by Major Patrick Ferguson had been badly defeated by an evenly matched patriot force under Colonel James Williams at King's Mountain, a ridge in the northwest corner of South Carolina, on the North Carolina border. As a result of the battle, all that area was under patriot control, so Cornwallis had fallen back to Winnsboro, South Carolina.

Greene, the strategist and tactician, saw in this situation his first big chance. He could not hope successfully to meet Cornwallis in open battle until his army was reorganized, supplied, and reinforced. But, by placing himself in a pivotal position, where he could threaten and harass, or retreat if he had to, he could force a period of inaction on the British commander. He could prevent the enemy from making any further moves northward or further terrorizing the inhabitants of South Carolina. And a breathing spell was vitally needed. By transferring his army from Charlotte, North Carolina, where low ground turned the camp into a millpond after every heavy rain, to a more defensible position, he could reorganize with less danger of attack. Koscuisko's pivot camp at Hick's Creek, near Cheraw, South Carolina, on the Pee Dee River, was chosen because it was one of the few highlands of the Carolinas.

Cornwallis, despite his retreat to Winnsboro after King's Mountain, felt himself in a strong position to pro-

THE WAR
IN THE
SOUTH

ROUTES OF CORNWALLIS ••••••••••••••••• ↝

tect his chain of interior forts—Camden on his right, Ninety Six at his left rear, covering the headwaters of the Saluda River, and Fort Granby below him at the confluence of the Saluda and the Congaree Rivers. Also below him were Fort Motte, at the junction of the Wateree and the Congaree, Fort Watson on the Santee River, and Orangeburg on the Edisto River, with Georgetown and Charleston on the seacoast. His communications with sea power at Charleston were secure. And he had a rich, fertile district at his rear from which to supply his troops.

The British lieutenant general had 3224 seasoned veterans, by his own count. Greene had almost 1000 men less, and most of them were militia. The combat readiness ratio thus actually stood at about four to one.

Up until now his lordship had all but conquered South Carolina. Georgia was within his grasp. Then North Carolina and Virginia would be easy conquests, and the American cause surely would be lost. What Howe had failed to do in the North—split the thirteen colonies down the middle by taking control of the Hudson River, Lake George, and Lake Champlain—Cornwallis might accomplish by cutting the new states in two from east to west. Greene's job was to prevent this maneuver and to recapture the South. But meanwhile he must have time to reorganize. He could buy this time only by taking a calculated risk to his army and to his own military reputation.

Before Greene set out on his relatively short march to

the Cheraw highlands on the Pee Dee River, he split his
forces and detached Old Dan Morgan with 300 of his best
troops and Colonel William Washington's light dragoons
on a special mission. Their orders were to take a position
in the western area of South Carolina beyond the Broad
River, where they would be at no great distance from
Cornwallis. There Morgan would be joined by 300 volun-
teers and up to 400 South Carolina and Georgia militia.

The move opened up a wide field of operations between
the Broad and Pacolet Rivers. The action threatened the
safety of the important posts at Ninety Six and Augusta to
the west, which was sure to alarm Cornwallis. And at the
same time Morgan threatened his lordship's own flank.

With the remainder of his forces, numbering 1100 men,
of whom only 650 were veteran Continentals, Greene took
his new post at Hick's Creek near Cheraw. When he arrived at the new base on December 26, 1780, he found
that Kosciusko had done a magnificent job in laying out
the camp. Its defenses were strong and food and forage
could be easily obtained in the area.

One of the immediate advantages of the Cheraw camp
was that it prevented Cornwallis from attempting to possess Crook Creek, which would give him command of the
greatest part of the provisions of "the lower country," as
Greene described it. The move also enabled Greene not
only to reorganize but to improve the health and discipline of his troops.

These daring and unorthodox tactics upset the British plans. At once Cornwallis found himself restricted to a much narrower area, with most of his supplies from the interior cut off. The drooping spirits of the patriots also were revived, and American recruiting stepped up as the men felt again that they had a chance to fight on more even terms. Besides, British communications with Charleston could be cut by the Americans at any time, and outlying British posts were in peril. Any British invasion farther northward was unthinkable until Greene's army was beaten.

This bold move, as Greene had foreseen, compelled Cornwallis to divide his own force. The British could not attack Greene, leaving Morgan unopposed behind them. If they did, Morgan might capture Ninety Six or Augusta, or both. And they could not pursue Morgan too far, or go north into Virginia, while Greene had "the whole country open" before him. For Greene was as near to Charleston as Cornwallis, and so he kept that key post with its garrison under constant threat. Greene also was in no immediate danger of being cut off himself from the reinforcements that he had every reason to expect soon would arrive from the North.

The uncertainty of Greene's movements indeed had forced the British to leave a large garrison in Charleston, thus cutting down Cornwallis's own field strength. However, Greene knew he could not hold the country below the falls of the Pee Dee River, because there were no defensible passes in the area. There were none, indeed, all the way "from the Chesapeake to Georgia." Below the falls all the rivers were deep, their banks covered with impassable swamps. The only crossings over these swamps were a few old and unreliable corduroy roads, made of logs laid crosswise. Greene felt he could not "afford to get tangled up among the difficulties they present" until he could "turn upon my enemy and fight him where I please."

Thus the two armies lay—three armies if Morgan's strong detached unit counted as one—watching, waiting, girding for the inevitable struggle that must follow for the control of all the southland and the fate of the United States.

The period was a trying one for Greene. Almost constantly he found himself having to settle disputes between troops of several states. Most contentious were the men of the Maryland line. Many of these men really had just grievances, and Greene understood, perhaps better than any other officer in the Army, the need for active sympathy, with which he strove to lighten their sufferings.

Nonetheless, Greene was a strict disciplinarian, the more so, perhaps, because of his long association with Baron von Steuben, who was still recruiting in Virginia. The baron had taught him the sheer necessity for discipline. Greene's amiable nature, even in dealing with subordinates, may have given some men in his new army the wrong impression, but they soon learned how tough he was under that appearance of geniality and relaxation. Men who had served under him for a long time knew of the finely tempered steel in his character. They did not need to be warned more than once.

But there were many among the Southern militia who felt that they still could come and go as they pleased. No regular Army commander could tolerate such a condition for long, even though partisan leaders such as Marion and Sumter were forced to do so. The men did not seem to think of their sudden leave-taking for home as desertion. They were merely going back to families who needed them.

Conditions became so serious that Greene was forced to issue general orders, warning his army that the next man who deserted would be hanged. Apparently there were men in the ranks who didn't believe Greene was that tough. But the next man who deserted was tried by court-martial, convicted, and hanged in the presence of the whole army. There were no more desertions. The men had learned that their new commander was determined to fashion a force that effectively could fight the British. And the first requisite of such an army was discipline.

So Greene soon won the respect and confidence of his men, especially since they already had learned that he was willing to share their discomforts. Morgan's army

soon reached a point between the Pacolet and the Broad
Rivers, some 140 miles from Greene's camp near Cheraw
on the Pee Dee River. Cornwallis planned his strategy to
meet this move. When expected reinforcements arrived
under Major General Alexander Leslie, his lordship was
determined to risk everything on a sudden drive between
Greene and Morgan. He would attack Morgan first, using
Colonel Banastre Tarleton's Green Dragoons, a highly
trained force of Tories and American deserters, the terror
of the southland, and other veteran units. Then he would
try to encircle Greene and defeat him.

Greene, however, had expected some such enemy tactic, knowing Cornwallis to be impatient and something of
a gambler. That possibility was one reason he had sent
Morgan around to outflank his lordship, dangerous and
militarily unorthodox as he knew the move to be.

Tarleton—young, reckless, courageous, but often lack-
ing in sound judgment—rose to the bait almost as soon as
Cornwallis told him to "go after Morgan." Never for a
moment did he let up on the Old Wagoner; he was bound
to crush Morgan or force him to disband his army.
Greene, meanwhile, waited with what patience he could
muster for the outcome of this new military chess game
that he had initiated. He spent the time building and
training his army and getting supplies and reinforcements. He also made careful plans for a hasty retreat if
putting water between himself and the enemy became
necessary.

Couriers kept up a constant flow of dispatches between Greene and Morgan over the 140 miles of mostly Tory country. The partisan leaders, Marion and Sumter, kept Greene well informed of Cornwallis's moves, and Morgan in the same way knew every move Tarleton made.

Tarleton's raids on the countryside had made his name the most hated in the South. He was cruel to a conquered enemy and seemed to delight in laying waste, with the two light cannon he carried with him, the districts occupied by Whigs, as the American patriots were called. Cornwallis, meanwhile, settled down at a place called Turkey Creek, not far from where Tarleton and Morgan were maneuvering.

Some forty miles northwest of Cornwallis's camp was a place called Cowpens, so named because for many years it had been used to house cattle during the summer grazing season. There, on the early morning of January 17, 1781, the Old Wagoner, with militiamen and a few trained Continentals, severely defeated Tarleton's trained troops. Frontier marksmanship proved too much for either Tarleton's cannon or his bayonets and cavalry to overcome. The red and green uniformed British ran from the field or laid down their arms. Most were captured. Morgan barely was able to prevent a wholesale massacre of the hated "Tarleton's Butchers."

Only Tarleton and the remnants of his shattered Green Dragoons escaped to Cornwallis's camp on Turkey Creek. The British lost 110 killed, 229 wounded, 800 prisoners, the two cannon, 800 muskets, 100 horses, their baggage train, ammunition, and "all the music," as Old Dan was happy to report to Greene. Morgan lost 12 killed and 61 wounded, which seemed to prove that the Americans were better marksmen than the British. Morgan, a "simple backwoodsman," had carried off one of the most masterly battles on this or any other continent.

By evening Morgan was across the Broad River, headed for the Little Catawba. Cornwallis waited for Leslie to come up, so that by the time his lordship reached the river he learned that Old Dan had crossed it two days earlier.

# 12

## Retreat to the North

★★★★★★★★★★★★★★

Then Cornwallis made a bad blunder. To speed his army, he burned his baggage train, all but a few wagons to carry ammunition, medical supplies, and the wounded.

Morgan was in such pain, at this point, from a recurrence of his chronic sciatica, that he scarcely could ride his horse at a walk. So that his army might make better time, he traveled on a supply wagon part of the way on the march to the Catawba. Both armies plodded through deep mud and incessant rain.

When Cornwallis reached the Catawba on January 30, he found Morgan already had crossed the river, which was so swollen by the heavy rains that the British could not hope to ford it. Cornwallis was forced to pitch camp and wait for the flood to subside.

Greene, fearing that Morgan's fast worsening physical condition might force him to leave the field, rode through the Tory-infested countryside from Cheraw with only one aide, over miry, rain-soaked roads and across badly swollen streams, to join Old Dan on the Catawba. The safety of Greene's mission to the South depended upon getting Morgan's little army away from Cornwallis, and Greene felt that he should be there to face his lordship personally at this crucial moment, if the Old Wagoner couldn't keep to the saddle.

Greene reached Morgan's camp on the Catawba on the very day Cornwallis pitched camp on the other side. "What of Cornwallis?" was Greene's first question of the Old Wagoner.

"He has destroyed his baggage," replied Morgan with a wide grin and a grim chuckle, belying his excruciating pain. "His lordship seems resolved to push through the country."

A little smile of excitement lighted Greene's blue eyes. Slapping one leg with his riding crop, he spread his hands in an expressive gesture and exclaimed, "Then he is ours!"

The general slid from the wet saddle and limped over to Morgan's command tent to a field desk and began to write urgent notes summoning the local militia leaders to bring in their men at once.

Since the militia reinforcements ought to be in camp by the time the Catawba receded, Greene decided to dispute passage of the river. With one more victory he might smash Cornwallis and end the campaign right there. But on the very day of Greene's arrival the river began to fall. The next day he gave up the idea of making a stand and ordered Morgan to fall back to Salisbury, North Carolina, near the Yadkin River. Greene himself remained behind to make one last appeal for more militiamen.

Cornwallis on February 1 determined to force passage of the ford, although the river at this point was five hundred yards wide and up to four feet deep. But the rain had started again and within a few hours the stream might not be passable. He could see the fires in the American camp across the river, little suspecting that they were a ruse. He supposed, of course, that Morgan's whole army still lay there, feeling secure behind the swollen stream. Instead, only a rear guard commanded by General William Davidson remained. Cornwallis hoped to make one swift, sure stroke that would end the war in the South. For if he could surprise Morgan and destroy his army, Greene later might be wiped out in the same way.

Darkness hid Cornwallis's men for the first half of the way as they led the van across the stream, holding their muskets and ammunition boxes high above their heads to keep them from getting wet. Then, in midstream, the American campfires threw a revealing light on the wading

British. Alert American sentries fired upon them. Soon men and horses were floundering under the steady and deadly American fire. Leslie's horse was carried well downstream. Cornwallis's horse was shot under him, but it managed to gain the farther bank, where it died. Brigadier General Charles O'Hara's horse rolled over with him.

Some of the British mistook the course of the ford when their guides fled under fire. The soldiers plunged straight ahead and thus missed the ambush that the American rear guard had set for them. In this way the enemy gained the farther bank and was able to turn the American flank. General Davidson was killed, and his men panicked and ran. Perhaps they could not be too much blamed for their flight, since they were caught between the fire of the British and the light of their own campfires, which made them prime targets.

Most of the militamen quietly faded into the surrounding woods, but those with horses fled to Tarrant's Tavern, half way to Salisbury, North Carolina.

Greene, still determined to round up as many local militiamen as he could persuade to join him, had set up temporary headquarters in a house not far from Tarrant's Tavern. He had sent word to General Huger, in temporary command of the main army at Cheraw, to rendezvous with Morgan's unit at Salisbury in the shortest possible marching time.

Already Greene had made plans to retreat across the Dan River into Virginia. There he would be nearer his supplies, which he had told Davie and Carrington to send ahead of Huger to safer locations in western Virginia. There, too, he would be nearer the reinforcements that he ordered von Steuben to send from Virginia. By the time the two units of the army formed a junction at Salisbury the big military storehouse there and another at Hillsboro, also in North Carolina, should be safely beyond the reach of the British.

Orders had gone out to Greene's quartermaster general to collect all the boats on the Dan River for miles upstream and downstream and to hold them in readiness at one point. From there they could be transferred quickly to whatever spot he chose for the reunited army to cross that strategic river into Virginia.

Seemingly, Greene had taken every possible precaution to protect his army and the hopes of redeeming the southland. But, even so, before starting out on his perilous journey to join Morgan, he wrote to his wife: "I am of Spanish disposition, always the most serious when there is the greatest run of good fortune, for fear of some ill-fated stroke."

As Greene waited vainly for recruits to flock to his standard he knew that his men were carrying out his orders. General Huger was hurrying with all speed, despite rain and frozen ground and nearly impassable roads, to the rendezvous at Salisbury. Morgan was well on the way to the Yadkin River. Added assurance lay in the fact that Marion was in command of Huger's rear guard.

Greene's quill pen was busy scratching out orders and messages as the hours wore on. Still it rained and the night was chilly. At midnight a mud-splattered messenger drew his horse to a sliding halt outside the little farmhouse and was ushered in to the commander. Greene leaned back in his chair, perfectly at ease but showing the strain of long hours without sleep. Only his big, kindly blue eyes searched the face of the messenger, waiting for the report. The fate of the country as well as of the South might hang on the man's words.

"Davidson is dead, sir. The militia has dispersed and Cornwallis is over the Catawba."

Greene's heart was heavy as, within a few minutes, he set out alone in the bone-chilling rain, heading his horse for Salisbury. There he had agreed to meet his good friend, Doctor Read.

He found Read waiting at Steele's Tavern in Salisbury.

"What," asked Read in surprise, "alone, General?"

For once the outwardly lighthearted and confident Greene betrayed his inner feelings. He threw a weary leg over his horse and slid to the ground. If ever a man of Greene's usually cheerful nature could be despondent, Greene was that night. He nodded. "Yes, Doctor, tired, hungry, alone, and penniless."

Quickly he was ushered into the tavern, where a bright fire had been kept ablaze for him, warming and cheering the room. He found that Mrs. Steele had a hot meal waiting, with a steaming hot drink. When Greene had eaten, he was more relaxed and, quite evidently, had regained some of his usual confidence.

Mrs. Steele, who had overheard his reply to Doctor Read, came close to the table, a small leather bag of hard money in either hand. "Take these, General. For you need them, and I can do without them."

Deeply touched at this patriotic gesture, Greene thanked her, accepting the gold as a loan that he would repay. Then, noticing a portrait of King George III on the taproom wall, he walked over to a nearby writing desk and dipped a quill pen in the inkhorn. Turning the portrait over so that the king faced the wall, he wrote on the back: "Hide thy face, George, and blush."

Greene's deep sense of humor and his confidence had returned to full flood. There was a brightness in his eyes again and a spring to his limping step as he ordered his horse and rode out into the night for Salisbury village, following Morgan's retreating men.

Cornwallis could not be more than a few miles behind him, which meant the British might catch Morgan with his back to the Yadkin River. But Cornwallis didn't know that Greene's specially built, shallow-draft boats were traveling with Morgan. The Old Wagoner could cross the

Yadkin, even if the river were in flood, but there would be
no boats available for the British. Greene had word that
his commissary officers had succeeded in collecting all of
them for American use.

Then a hitch developed in Greene's plans, one possibility even the usually thorough Greene had overlooked.
When Morgan reached Salisbury with word that Cornwallis was hard on his heels, many of the residents packed
up what belongings they could load onto small carts or
carriages and trudged after the rear of Morgan's men.
They were not going to remain behind and take their
chances with the enemy. This traffic slowed up the rear,
but by evening all but three wagons, a few fugitives, and
Morgan's rear guard were over the river, thanks to
Greene's foresight in providing his own portable ferry and
in confiscating what few other boats were available. The
British advance guard caught up with those not over the
river, and there was a short, sharp fight, but the last of the
fugitives and the guard were ferried over before Cornwallis's main army arrived early in the morning.

The Americans were safe on the farther side, in plain
sight. Cornwallis, without boats, once again had been
deprived of a quick victory and was forced to pitch camp
and wait, so wild and swift was the flooded river that
separated the two armies.

But there was one thing Cornwallis could do; he unlimbered his artillery and began to shell the American camp.

The topography, however, protected the Americans, and most of the British cannonballs failed to inflict damage.

When, because of bad weather, General Huger could not rendezvous at Salisbury in time, Greene ordered him to march instead to Guilford Courthouse. This little hamlet lay between the Deep and Haw Rivers.

Since there was no danger that Cornwallis could cross the Yadkin until the river subsided, Greene set up a field headquarters in a small cabin and went to work on his dispatches. Hour after hour the general's pen scratched. Only now and then did he stop as an orderly ushered in an officer. Then Greene laid down his pen, stretched out his legs, slid back in his chair, folded his hands across his chest, and listened completely relaxed. When the necessary order had been given and the officer had gone, the general resumed his busy writing. He was utterly disregardful of the bombardment. Finally, clapboards were flying and the little building shook as an occasional cannonball bounced off the roof. Still Greene paid no attention. When he was interrupted by a visitor he listened attentively, his answers coming in as calm and deliberate a tone as though all was peace and quiet outside.

Cornwallis's spies had told him that the Americans could not possibly collect boats on the Dan River to effect a retreat into Virginia. So he decided that as soon as his men could ford the Yadkin he would go after Morgan and catch him surely this time with his back to the Dan. Then he would turn on the main American army and smash it, too.

Greene broke camp and set off with Morgan's army, heading for Guilford Courthouse on February 8, 1781. Meanwhile, Lighthorse Harry Lee's Legion had made contact with Huger's main army. The two forces joined under Greene at Guilford on February 9, and Greene briefly thought of turning to fight Cornwallis when he should come up. The terrain favored the American army, but since the expected militia recruits had failed to come, offering battle would have been madness. The enemy had 3000 veteran troops; Greene had 2000 men, of whom only 1426 were dependable regulars.

Both sections of the army were tired on that raw February morning when General Huger and Harry Lee led their long train of human misery to a halt to join Morgan's men at Guilford Courthouse. The men were in rags. Some were barefoot; others wore shoes that were all but soleless. Some had tied old bags to their feet. The wheels on some of the supply wagons leaned to one side as though they would fall off any second. Most of the axles squealed for lack of grease. The horses' ribs stuck out; their harness was broken and mended. The sight was sad for Greene, but he was not dispirited. His army was whole. He still could choose to fight or to retreat. Having the initiative was what mattered, and he had it.

# 13

## Hare and Hounds to the Dan

★ ★ ★ ★ ★ ★ ★ ★ ★ ★ ★ ★ ★ ★

Greene decided to fall back at once, but slowly, on his supply bases and expected reinforcements north of the Dan River. The decision was a bold one.

His campaign thus far had been quite satisfactory. He had taken the initiative from Cornwallis, he had kept the Tories from flocking to Cornwallis's banner as they had been expected to do, and, above all, his resourceful retreat had kept his whole army "in being," giving heart to the patriots of the countryside. This encouragement was most important if the spirit of rebellion was to be kept alive in the South.

Sumter was back in the field after recovering from a

wound and was rallying the South Carolina militia, far to the south. Marion had been ordered, after serving as Huger's rear guard, to recross the Santee River and harass the enemy. Davie and Carrington were with Greene again, thus relieving him of double duty of commanding general and serving as his own quartermaster general. Many a day and night he hadn't taken off his clothes, and if he got four hours sleep in forty-eight hours he was lucky.

More important than anything else, Greene had eluded the best-laid traps of Lord Cornwallis and led his men into a country where the living and foraging were better. His army had greater confidence in him than ever.

What troubled Greene at this time was not so much the remaining distance to the Dan River, which he must cross before Cornwallis could get there first and cut him off, but the conditions under which his reunited army must march. The February roads—and most of them were not worth the name in that backwoods, red-clay region—were deep and slimy in the daytime under the sun's melting rays, but froze at night in sharp unevenness after the pounding of foot and hoof. The going was hard on both men and horses in each army. The difference was that the British were well clothed, although they were marching without wagon and baggage.

A very real danger existed that the traitor, Benedict Arnold, now a British major general and raiding a part of the Virginia countryside, might link up with Cornwallis and try to pin Greene down between them. There was a reason for deep anxiety and Greene had his moments of doubt, but he never showed them.

"My hopes rest on my knowledge of your talents," Washington wrote. The Northern army as well as the people of the South were waiting anxiously for the result of this cat and mouse game that Cornwallis was trying to play with Greene. Up to then Greene had turned it around, so that he was the cat. The maneuvering for position went on while Cornwallis rested his men, preparing them for a quick, bold push northward.

If he could corner Greene with his back to the Dan River, the war in the South would be over, perhaps the war in all of North America. This event would happen if the stream, with all the rain, proved too swollen to ford. If not, Cornwallis only had to follow fast enough to catch Greene's little army as it struggled across the river, encumbered by wagons and baggage, and annihilate it. Either way Greene would be forced to surrender. Cornwallis saw himself as the hero of Britain.

Greene sent his baggage and all unnecessary equipment northward to safety. He made careful plans to set the people harassing the British rear and cutting off their supplies. Word came that his order to collect all the boats on the Dan River for miles up and down the stream had been carried out to the letter. The boats could be brought quickly to any given point for a crossing. Then he made a forced march toward a place on the Dan known as Boyd's Crossing.

First another fateful decision had to be made, and again Greene threw out the rule book. That Cornwallis should not discover, until too late, where the American army was to cross the Dan was absolutely essential. There was only one way to do so, and it was to create a diversion and hope that Cornwallis would be deceived by it.

Greene detached 700 picked men—toughest in physique, the best shots, the most loyal—under Colonel Otho Williams with orders to throw themselves deliberately in front of Cornwallis. Knowing how to pick men was another of Greene's qualities that made him a great leader. Command of this daring expedition was offered first to Dan Morgan, but the Old Wagoner was suffering so greatly from rheumatism that he had to go home, with Greene's thanks for his long service.

Williams put the infantry under Colonel John Eager Howard, of Maryland, whose cool, deliberate courage made him useful in decisive moments. Lee commanded the cavalry detachment, which included his Legion. This special group took the field February 10, the day after the two units of the army had effected a junction at Guilford.

Soon Cornwallis's scouts saw a considerable body of infantry and horse ahead of the advancing British army. His lordship at once supposed, as Greene had intended, that the whole American army was retreating just ahead of him, headed for the Dan. Cornwallis tightened up his straggling line and urged his men forward as fast as the bad roads permitted.

If the British leader noticed, after a time, that the Americans were veering to the left somewhat, he apparently thought nothing of the fact. But it was part of the plan. Cornwallis was to be drawn far enough west of the main body of Americans so that Greene and Williams could march in almost parallel columns. They would not be so far apart that Cornwallis, if he discovered what had happened could attack first one and then the other and destroy them. So the earl was racing toward the Dan River with Greene on his right and Williams a little ahead on his left, never suspecting the trick that was being played upon him!

Cornwallis was sure that Greene would attempt to cross on the shallow fords of the upper Dan, where even the spring freshets would not present too much of a problem. His lordship was determined to get there first or quickly enough to prevent the Americans from crossing.

The light troops led by Williams thus effectively masked the movement of Greene's main army as both Americans and British toiled over the alternately miry and frozen red-clay country roads. While Williams led Cornwallis ever slightly to the left, Greene kept his main body straight ahead on the main road to where his boats awaited him. His men, of necessity, paid a high price in suffering for the swift-paced march. Many of them, the soles of their shoes worn through in the rough country, left bloody footprints on the broken and frosty ground. Others snatched what few fitful hours of sleep they could on the bare ground, cold and chilled to the bone, without blankets.

Sometimes three men shivered under one thin blanket. Their commander was even worse off. Greene spent most of the nights writing appeals for aid and men, making out reports, and preparing plans for the next day. When at last he had a little time for sleep often his asthma kept him awake. But through the weary march he seemed to be everywhere, to know everything that was going on. And his men responded by giving that extra ounce of effort that in any battle often spells the difference between victory and defeat. They, too, were determined to reach and cross the Dan ahead of Cornwallis. This thought seemed to warm them a little, even as their small bivouac fires of green wood more often smouldered than burned. The fires gave off less than enough heat to dry their clothing, wet through after wading swollen creeks and small feeder streams.

Soon many of the North Carolina militiamen deserted. They could see no point in leaving their unprotected families so far behind, with the British known to be closely following and undoubtedly raiding the countryside. Greene could not blame the men too much, and trying to round up and hang every man who deserted under such conditions was unthinkable. Besides, he had only one objective: to reach the Dan ahead of Cornwallis.

Greene showed his deep concern in a note to Williams: "You have the flower of the army. Do not expose the men too much, lest our situation grow more critical."

Greene also gave Williams explicit instructions to "follow our route" so as not to divide the two forces by more than a few miles. He had to be in a position to recall his 700 picked men and be sure they could reach him within a short time, especially since, he told Williams, he had reason to believe that "one of Tarleton's officers was in our camp night before last."

Williams was doing a good job of deceiving the enemy while keeping his men as well protected as he could by distance. Cornwallis was more convinced than ever that he was pursuing Greene's whole army. "And I have him in my grasp," he gleefully wrote.

General O'Hara led Cornwallis's advance. Lee protected Williams's rear. But so close was the British vanguard that Williams, to make certain there would be no surprise attack, posted double guards every night. The light infantrymen took turns, half standing duty while the other half slept. Six hours allowance for sleep in forty-eight was the rule.

For three days Cornwallis pursued. Most of the time O'Hara was within musket shot of Lee's Legion, and Cornwallis thought that he was headed straight for the spot where Greene would try to cross the more shallow fords of the Dan! Lower down the fords would be too deep to wade as the river was in a raging spring flood.

What Cornwallis still didn't know was that Greene's boats already had been assembled on the banks of the Dan. Kosciusko and Carrington had done their work thoroughly. There wasn't a boat to be had by the British for many miles along the south bank of the river. And on the north bank Kosciusko already had completed strong earthworks. Behind them, Greene's army could compel Cornwallis to pay a heavy price in killed and wounded if he tried to force passage for himself and his men.

On the third day, Tarleton pushed forward to attack Lee. There was a brief, sharp fight between the two crack cavalry units. The British lost eighteen killed, the Americans two, and Tarleton quickly broke off the engagement. At about this time Cornwallis finally discovered that he had been tricked. Immediately he changed his route of march and pushed his men even faster in an attempt to reach the lower Dan crossings ahead of Williams and Greene.

The outcome was a question of speed, and both Williams and his lordship bent every effort to gain the main objective. Shots frequently were exchanged between Lee and Tarleton, but there was no further attempt at a close encounter. Almost constantly the two forces were within sight of each other.

Cornwallis could not stop, even at night. There were only brief rests for his men to eat hastily prepared rations. It was cold, windy, and dark as Williams's men slogged on, the enemy ever closer upon their heels.

Suddenly a great light brightened the sky ahead. Quickly the word raced through the American ranks that it was the bivouac fires of Greene's main army, camped on the south side of the Dan. Something had gone amiss, and, if so, the men of Williams's brigade must stand and fight Cornwallis, giving their compatriots time to cross the river. They would be outnumbered at least four to one.

Just as quickly the American advance guard brought back word that the lights indeed were American camp-fires, but they were fires left carefully tended for the use of Williams's men when they should arrive. Williams was two days behind Greene! The men's loud cheers were heard by Cornwallis, who wondered what they meant. Williams made camp, for his troops were exhausted. Cornwallis, too, was forced to delay to give his own tired men some respite. But not for long. By midnight the British were on the march again, driving in Williams's mounted sentinels and proceeding at the double where the nature of the terrain permitted. Williams was forced to beat a hasty retreat, almost within sight of the enemy.

One more day, thought Cornwallis! One more day, and the war in North America will be over!

The night was dark, the cold was bone-chilling. Frost

covered the badly upheaved road. Men shivered as they marched, but most of them were cheerful. Whatever the outcome of the almost certain battle the next day, the end was near.

Otho Williams shared this belief even more certainly, and he was worried. He was determined to stand and fight, if such a move would save Greene's main army, although to do so meant either ultimate surrender or annihilation. What had happened?

Dawn came slowly. Each army halted for a brief, hastily prepared breakfast. Scarcely had Williams given the order to march on, an hour later, when a mud-splattered rider pulled his horse to a sliding stop at Williams's feet, saluted, and handed the young commander a dispatch. "General Greene's compliments, sir," the dispatch rider reported.

Greene had written: "The greater part of our wagons are over, and the troops are crossing."

Williams told his men, amid ringing volleys of cheers. The British advance must have heard the cheering and wondered what news could so inspire men who faced certain capture or death. Cornwallis pushed his men still harder.

All day the two armies struggled along the rutty road, stopping only for brief rests. Cornwallis was certain he had Greene boxed in now, even though he had been following only a diversionary force. Just ahead the two

American armies would join, with their backs to the river, and they could not escape.

Evening came, and another mud-splattered courier dashed up to Williams, handing him a dispatch from Greene: "Irvin's Ferry, 5½ o'clock. All our troops are over, and the stage is clear. The infantry will cross here, the horse below."

Riflemen and artillery, Greene wrote, had been posted behind Kosciusko's newly built earthworks to cover Williams's crossing by boat. "And I am ready to receive and give you a hearty welcome!" Those little extra touches of consideration and appreciation, such as that last phrase, were what endeared Greene as a commander to his men. Always he had an instinctive regard for the rights and feelings of others.

Otho Williams's tired face relaxed into a smile and his erect, military carriage seemed to stiffen in the saddle as he turned to his men and gave them the good news. Loud cheers from the American ranks must have surprised Cornwallis even more than the previous outbursts. But when, hours later, the Green Dragoons reached the Dan River, they found every American safely over and not a boat to be had on the south bank!

The broad and raging Dan River flowed between the two armies as the Americans enjoyed their best sleep in many days. Cornwallis's campfires dotted the night on the south bank. Greene, with his usual imagination and thoroughness, had foreseen every hazard in his more than 200-mile retreat from Cheraw, South Carolina.

Greene was busy again far into the night. Among his other chores was a report to Washington. "Our army is in good spirits," he wrote.

That comment was an understatement. His retreat of more than 200 miles into Virginia has been called one of the most masterly in history. Even Tarleton later would write: "Every measure of the Americans during their march to Virginia was judiciously designed and vigorously executed."

# 14

## Hide and Seek
★ ★ ★ ★ ★ ★ ★ ★ ★ ★ ★ ★ ★ ★

Cornwallis was checkmated. Even if he could have forded the Dan River, the American earthworks, with expert marksmen and cannon behind them, would have stopped him. He could not feed his army where he was, so he pulled back to Hillsboro, North Carolina. It was in Tory country, and he could count on some support there. He was pleased when enthusiasts, muskets in hand, flocked to his camp. Then the stream of Loyalists suddenly tapered off, much to his lordship's disgust and anger. He could not understand why.

In his bitterness the earl wrote that he was "amongst timid friends and adjoining inveterate rebels." He had blasted the Tories to the southward as "dastardly and pusillanimous" for deserting him earlier. Still, he was inclined to give these North Carolina Loyalists a chance to show their colors.

But Cornwallis knew he hadn't much time. His army needed supplies, including ammunition, from his nearest base, Wilmington, North Carolina, on the coast. And he rightly suspected that Greene had figured such desperation would force the British to retreat from Hillsboro to Wilmington. Such a retreat would invite harassing tactics by Greene that could annihilate the British army before it ever reached the coast.

Worst of all, Cornwallis already had written to King George III that the Carolinas were safe for the crown and that Georgia was pacified. The situation looked as though his lordship would be held accountable not only for losing the South but for raising false hopes in London of a quick ending to the war. Under such circumstances, the earl could not be blamed for permitting his gambler's instincts to temper his caution as a strategist and tactician. He was reckless.

The Rhode Island ironmaster, as his lordship liked to think of his rival across the Dan River, had no such misgivings. Greene was disappointed that expected reinforcements had not yet arrived from the North, but he was confident they would come in due time. Meanwhile, he had to keep Cornwallis off balance.

Andrew Pickens and Harry Lee were sent over the Dan

with a chosen force to harry Cornwallis, cut his communications, seize his supplies, and frighten the Tories into remaining at home. Greene realized that while the British commander probably wouldn't risk crossing the Dan with his present force, even though they were veterans, he might do so if enough Tories joined his ranks. Greene was playing for time to allow his reinforcements to come in, his supplies to arrive from the North, and more ammunition to be procured.

One thing worried him: Lee and Pickens, in their enthusiasm, might overreach themselves and get too far out of touch. Worse still, they might be surprised and captured or their band annihilated. He wanted to make certain that his orders would be carried out to the letter. So, close on their heels, he crossed the Dan himself, riding some eighteen miles south of the river. At a conference he told Lee and Pickens that he had decided to move his entire army south of the river within a few days. Then he wrapped himself in Pickens's blanket, caught a few hours' sleep on the bare ground, and well before daybreak was back over the Dan in his own camp.

The incident leaked out and spread through the American camp, giving the men ever greater confidence in their chief. For Greene's readiness to share the fatigue and poor food with his men was what they appreciated as much as his careful planning, vigilance, and caution. In an army of that kind this attitude was doubly important.

While Greene still was at the Lee-Pickens camp over

the Haw River, south of the Dan, a report was received
that Tarleton's Green Dragoons had been seen in the
vicinity. Greene rightly suspected that Tarleton's mission
was to drum up recruits among the Tories. Since prevent-
ing this recruitment was vital to Greene's plans, he ordered immediate pursuit of Tarleton. Lee and Pickens set
off at once. The Tories had to be taught that neither
Cornwallis nor Tarleton could protect them.

Lee and Pickens followed a trail of smoking farmhouses
that told where Tarleton or Tories marching to join
Cornwallis had passed. By noon the next day, while covering a wide area between the Haw and Deep Rivers, Lee
and Pickens nearly suprised Tarleton dining at a Tory
farmhouse, but he escaped.

A Tory named Pyles, who had the title of colonel, was
leading 300 men of the Haw and Deep Rivers' country,
looking for Tarleton, when two of Pyles's scouts fell in
with an officer of Lee's Legion, riding patrol some distance ahead of the unit. Lee's Legion and Tarleton's dragoons both dressed in smartly cut green uniforms. To most
people they looked alike. Pyles's men, having been told
that Tarleton was in the vicinity, as indeed he was, mistook Lee's officer for one of Tarleton's men. The quick-
witted American officer went along with the deception
and escorted Pyles's scouts to Lee. Equally quick-witted,
Lee, answering their greetings of "Colonel Tarleton, sir,"
questioned the men closely. He discovered that no one in
the group ever had seen Banastre Tarleton.

How much more emphatic, Lee thought, to teach the Tories a lesson by capturing them without a fight. They would learn that Cornwallis, indeed, was no protection, which was what Greene wanted. Lee ordered his column forward, posing as Tarleton, and soon caught up with Pyles who had stopped on a narrow, thickly wooded road to rest his mounted men and horses.

When Pyles's two scouts, or vedettes, rode in with Lee and introduced him as Colonel Tarleton, Pyles was overjoyed. He thought he had reached the safety of a trained unit of British horse much sooner than he had hoped. For there was no telling what might happen to his little band if they fell in with Greene. Of course, Greene was supposed to be north of the Dan, but who knew where that wily Rhode Islander ever was?

Lee had formed an instant plan to get his Legion ahead of the mounted Tories. Then, with Pickens's infantrymen behind them, the enemy would have no choice but to surrender. His horsemen began to pass the Tory line. But as Lee rode forward to exchange a handclasp with Colonel Pyles—still carrying out his masquerade—some quick eye on the Tory left, near Pyles's rear, spotted the well-known green twig of the Whig or patriot riflemen. The frightened Tory fired his musket. The shot went wild, but it had alarmed the Tories.

There was no chance to avoid a fight. With the two bodies of bitter enemies face to face, the first to strike probably would win. There would be no second chance.

Lee did not hesitate. "Draw sabers!" He didn't have to give the order to attack. Within seconds the heavy swords were slashing at Tory heads, cutting men down from their saddles before they could aim their muskets. Within minutes, 90 of the 300 Tories lay dead on the road. Most of the others, including Pyles, were wounded but managed to flee. Lee did not pursue them far. The stories they would tell throughout the countryside would do what Greene wanted, they would frighten the Tories into deserting Cornwallis.

And so it happened. The Whig Massacre, as Pyles's men described Lee's sudden attack, quickly terrorized the Tory community. The recruits who had been intent on joining Cornwallis decided to stay home and get their spring work done around the farm.

Meanwhile, Cornwallis, told by his spies that Greene had been seen south of the Dan, supposed that he must have his army with him. His lordship called in Tarleton—sending three couriers for him, to make certain that his order was obeyed—broke camp on the Haw River, crossed to the south side on February 27, and took a new post on a tributary, the Alamance River.

Greene was in motion even earlier, for on February 23 he had led his army south of the Dan, with the reinforcements that had arrived from Baron von Steuben in Virginia. Greene was determined to fight Cornwallis the moment he felt strong enough. Meanwhile he would trust

to the "resources of his fertile mind" to hold his ground. A
test of military strategy and tactical skill resulted that has
been called one of the most remarkable feats of Greene's
campaign in the South.

The Haw River communicates with Wilmington, but
halfway to the sea its name becomes the Cape Fear River.
The headwaters of the Haw form two adjacent triangles.
The northern tributary is Troublesome Creek, the southern is the Alamance River, and the central branch is
Reedy Fork. The usual crossing place on Troublesome
Creek was High Rock Ford. Cornwallis lay in camp on the
Alamance River, the southernmost of these main tribu-
taries of the Haw. If he were to conquer North Carolina
he had to destroy Greene's army. Most immediately, he
had to hold the Tories in line, intercept Greene's reinforcements and supplies from the North, and, if possible,
compel Greene to fight where he would be at a disadvan-
tage in numbers and ground. Only a few miles separated
the two armies.

Greene's problem was that he had to wait for still more
reinforcements before he would be strong enough to fight
a pitched battle. He must hold his communications open
to the North and so frighten the Tories that they would
not help Cornwallis. Keeping the way open to Virginia
required the utmost vigilance to prevent the enemy from
flanking him and attacking him from the rear. He knew
that in crossing south of the Dan he had put himself in an

extremely dangerous position, but he felt he could not wait longer to move. If he sat safely behind the shelter of the Dan, Cornwallis would have succeeded in recruiting enough Tories to make a frontal assault possible, however costly it might be in Tory lives.

Greene chose an area between Troublesome Creek and Reedy Fork for his operations during the next few weeks. It allowed considerable room for a maneuver. He could threaten Cornwallis, but at the same time he had an escape route back over the Haw and, if necessary, over the Dan into Virginia.

Determined to keep Cornwallis constantly off balance until he could give battle in the open, Greene changed position almost every night and never remained in one spot more than two nights. He had detailed information from spies of every movement of the enemy, but knowing what Greene planned was difficult for the British. And no wonder, for none but Greene knew on any day where his army would camp that night until the order to make camp was given, near nightfall. There was no chance whatever of a traitor or a spy divulging plans. And there were no written orders of troop movements that might fall into the hands of Cornwallis. Greene had complete confidence in his own judgment, and so he held no councils of war. Those methods together with the skill acquired by long experience, his energy, and promptness in exploiting a sudden advantage always yielded results.

"Good intelligence," Greene wrote to Washington, "is the soul of the army," and Greene's partisan allies provided it.

Nor could Cornwallis surprise Greene, for Williams's light troops had been thrown out again, and they were operating between Greene's main forces and the British. As Greene knew, Otho Williams was always on the alert.

After a day of hard work, mostly spent in the saddle, Greene retired to his tent to write dispatches. Tired out, he at length pulled off his long cavalry boots and stretched out on his camp bed for a nap, fully dressed. But long before the first streaks of dawn appeared he was out, visiting every sentry post, checking over the army. Many a weary and sleepy sentry got a word of cheer and a clap on the shoulder from "the General" as he waited in the chill hour before dawn for his relief. The army knew that while most men could sleep, their commanding general almost never did, and then only briefly.

Early one morning Greene happened to pass the tent of a Virginia colonel who was snoring loudly. Greene went in and, placing a hand on the colonel's shoulder, gently awakened him. "Good heavens, Colonel, how can you sleep with the enemy so near, and this the very hour for surprise?" It was too dark for the colonel to see the amusement in Greene's eyes, but he grinned and replied, "Why, General, I knew that *you* were awake!"

Greene thought this retort the best compliment he had received during the entire war, all the more because, from the day he left the camp on the Pee Dee River a month before to join Morgan, he never had taken off his clothes to sleep. He had changed them, of course, but always he had thrown himself, nearly exhausted, on his camp cot fully dressed, except for his boots. He never knew what minute he might have to be up.

The movement of Williams's light infantry was timed with that of the main army. One day Greene would move as though to form a junction with Williams; next day he would fall back on Troublesome Creek or to Reedy Fork; then suddenly he would reappear in some other area. To the terrified Tories, who were always menaced from a different quarter, several armies seemed to be moving at the same time over the little triangle. This strategy kept them properly subdued so that few of them dared to join Cornwallis. The time was not right to declare themselves either for or against the king or the United States. They hung up their muskets and attended strictly to their farm work, as Greene had intended they should. Cornwallis, meanwhile, was getting no recruits. His foraging parties were harassed by Williams, Lee, and Pickens. Even his personal baggage would have been captured one night by the Americans, except that the men lost their way in the dark near the enemy camp. Lee constantly hovered over the British, and every effort of Tarleton to capture him was foiled by the Virginia cavalryman's alertness.

Eagerly Cornwallis watched for a chance to surprise Greene. Once, in a heavy early morning fog, he tried to bag Williams's band, but the American scouts were too wary for him. Greene was warned by mounted courier that Cornwallis was on the march.

There was skillful maneuvering by both sides and some sharp, brief skirmishes, including one that took a heavy toll at Wetzel's Mills on Reedy Fork. Then Cornwallis gave up the effort, falling back to rest his men at Bell's Mills on Deep River, to the south.

Greene wrote to Governor Thomas Jefferson of Virginia, realizing that he had been sharply criticized for retreating so much: "Nothing shall hurry me into a measure that is not suggested by prudence or connects with the interest of the Southern department."

At last heavier reinforcements arrived—militia from North Carolina and Virginia and 400 newly trained Continentals who had enlisted for eighteen months' service. With them Greene had enough men. On March 10, 1781, he dissolved Williams's special light force, integrating it into a reorganized army, and sped by forced marches to Guilford Courthouse. He was determined to give battle or, if Cornwallis refused to fight, to go after him.

Battle had become a military necessity for both generals. Cornwallis, without the wagon train he had burned in his pursuit of Morgan a few weeks before had run low on ammunition and his nearest supply was in Wilmington. His food was also running low, for even in Tory country he had not been able to forage well, and often American raiders captured what was gathered.

Worse than any problem for Cornwallis, except the low supply of ammunition, was the increasing number of desertions. His men were willing enough to stand up to an enemy in battle, but cold, hunger, wornout shoes, and long marches in the night were too much for them to take. Unlike the Americans, they were not fighting for their homes and independence. Some of the British regulars even deserted directly to the American camp. Even men in the elite British Guards had gone over to Greene. And without decisive victory Cornwallis feared he could not depend upon the further loyalty of the Tories.

For Greene, while a battle was vital, it was not all or nothing as with Cornwallis. Greene felt that a sharp, decisive blow might cripple the British by encumbering Cornwallis with many wounded. Then, stunned and bleeding, he would be forced to retreat down the Haw and Cape Fear Rivers to Wilmington, harried all the way.

The American army numbered 4243 infantry, with 161 cavalry, a total of 4404. Of these troops only 1490 were dependable Continentals; the others were militia. But, even if half the militia were to run in a fight, they were almost certain to stand long enough to fire two or three rounds for each man. The Continentals, being trained and tough, could handle the rest of the job. Moreover, the

American cavalry was known to surpass the British in both number and quality. The worst that could befall Greene, he decided, was loss of the battlefield and the dispersal of his militia. But he could compel Cornwallis to retreat to the coast. The Americans, if necessary, only would have to retreat to the other side of the Dan, regroup, and try again.

During these anxious days, Greene had the quiet joy of knowing that a second son, named Nathanael, after his father, had been born on January 27, 1781, in the Coventry home. How he wished he might return to Rhode Island soon, even for one day, to see his beloved Caty and his four children together.

# 15

## Guilford Courthouse
★★★★★★★★★★★★★★

Guilford Courthouse, in North Carolina, was an ideal spot for Greene to give battle to Cornwallis. The area was sparsely settled, and the high road south to Salisbury cut through it.

The courthouse stood on the brow of a hill, backed by smaller rises of ground. At the bottom of the half-mile-long, gently sloping hill a little brook rippled through a thick forest. Fields had been planted to corn adjacent to the courthouse. The country was open, good for the deployment of troops. Long narrow corn fields extended along both sides of the Salisbury road, which ran up the hill, and on the side of the road from which the enemy must come lay a swamp and the little rivulet that fed it.

The whole area was naturally defended by broken ravines between the series of hills and abounded in strong positions.

Greene figured there never might be a better chance to face Cornwallis, and, liking the advantage of Guilford Courthouse as a battlefield, he broke camp on March 14, 1781, and reached the village in the afternoon. There still was light enough to make another survey of the field.

"Do not expose yourself needlessly," Greene's aides pleaded the night before the battle. "Put our lives at every hazard, but be careful of your own. If we fall, our loss will not be felt, but your death not only would be fatal to the army, but in all probability greatly retard, if not destroy, every hope of securing independence of the South."

Greene acknowledged their concern with thanks, but he made no promises. He knew how hard keeping them would be. Dashing to a spot where he was most needed, either to give directions or to cheer his men, was so natural for him that his aides knew they probably had made a vain plea.

That night the American army slept on the battlefield, hopeful and cheerful. Tomorrow would be the testing for which they all had waited and suffered so many weeks!

The day dawned bright and clear. A light frost quickly melted. The air was bracing, despite the chill, with the exhilarating freshness of spring. The weather was a cheerful augury, and the men were confident; their spirits soared. They ate a tranquil breakfast around their morning campfires.

Lighthorse Harry Lee, meanwhile, was out scouting in the no man's land to the south between the two armies. Soon a courier dashed in with word to Greene that Cornwallis was on the march. Towards noon there came the sound of firing. Another courier brought word to Greene that Tarleton briefly had engaged Lee, leaving behind several empty British saddles.

Greene at once drew up his troops in line of battle, but his objective still was not necessarily to gain an outright victory. If he could crush the enemy in this battle, well and good, but he would not put his own army in Cornwallis's power by overextending himself.

The Americans were drawn up in three lines, presenting three successive barriers to the enemy. Each line would have to be overcome before the one behind it could be attacked. Or so Greene supposed.

The first line was placed at the skirt of the wood, with open ground in front of its center and with its flanks extending into the cover. Fences still were standing in the cornfields nearby, forming a kind of breastworks behind which militiamen fought best. If they could stand and fire several rounds before giving way, dangerous gaps might be torn in the enemy lines. Greene had little faith in raw militia, but he felt they could, even within a short time, do much damage to the foe with their skilled marksmanship. Also, two light pieces of artillery were stationed in advance of them.

Three hundred yards farther back, in the midst of the wood, was the second line. It, too, consisted chiefly of militia. But mixed in with these men were seasoned Virginia Continentals, doing militia duty as substitutes from their state. Both lines extended across the road. These veterans were present because Greene urgently had requested Governor Jefferson to send them to stiffen the backbone of his militiamen in their first battle contact.

If both the seasoned Virginians and the more seasoned North Carolinians in the second line held for only a short while, their marksmanship might demoralize and break even the trained British regulars. The third and main line was composed of Continentals under General Huger and Colonel Otho Williams. These men were placed in the open ground around the courthouse, about 400 yards in the rear of the second line, and on the right of the road from Salisbury in a double front. But of these trained troops, there was only one veteran regiment. William Washington's dragoons and Colonel Charles Lynch's riflemen were posted on the left flank, with Lee's Legion, the flower of the army, on the right flank. Both flanking corps were hidden in woods.

The day was hot, and Greene wiped perspiration from his ample forehead with one hand, as he rode along the line, holding his hat with the other. In a clear and firm voice he called his men's attention to the strength of their position and asked of the men in the first ranks for "only three rounds. Three rounds, my boys, and then you can fall back!" At last he took his position with the Continentals, ready to go wherever he might be needed most.

Cornwallis formed his men in one line, with no reserve, the usual British tactic, in open contempt of the Americans as fighting men. Leslie held his right, with the Seventy-first British regiment, the German regiment of Bose, and the First battalion of the Guards, while on the left were posted the Twenty-third and Thirty-third regiments, the Grenadiers, and another battalion of the Guards. In the woods on the left of his artillery were yagers, armed with short-barreled, large-bore rifles, and light infantry of the Guards. Tarleton's cavalry, in column, was ordered not to attack without positive orders from Cornwallis.

Cornwallis rushed almost at once to the attack, even in the face of the American artillery fire and of his men's fatigue from marching. Soon the battle became general. Greene's militia, as he expected, fled under British point-blank fire and a bayonet charge, but the American flankers held firm. They gave the Virginians time to open up on the British with the coolness of veterans and the precision of practiced marksmen.

Symptoms of uneasiness began almost at once to appear in the charging British line, but discipline held the redcoats together, and they pressed forward with the bayonet. Great gaps in their line developed, thanks to the deadly volleys of the Americans. Soon, under such a withering fire, the British veterans were in a panic. The next few minutes Greene thought, held the promise of a sure victory. Quickly he rode along the line of the Continentals, exhorting them to be firm and give the enemy the finishing blow.

Then, for the first time, discipline met discipline as more British veterans charged head on into Virginians and Marylanders. The Americans poured in a well-directed fire, and, before the stunned and confused British could recover from the shock, Greene's men themselves fixed bayonets and charged.

Quickly and almost unbelievably, the British route was all but complete. Had the American cavalry been near enough at hand to follow up the infantry's blow, or had Greene dared to bring forward his one reserve regiment, the fate of the day would have been decided. But the veteran regiment of Continentals was the core of the army in the South. He could not risk these men at that point, and he was wise. For an American regiment broke and fled, weakening the whole line, but it held when William Washington's cavalry came thundering up, charged, and broke the enemy ranks. Colonel John Eager Howard's Marylanders followed up the calvary charge with the bayonet, giving the enemy no time to regroup.

Cornwallis's horse had been shot from under him, and

the British general barely escaped capture. In desperation his lordship, much to the distress of General Charles O'Hara, opened fire with his cannon upon some of his own men in an effort to stop the Americans. Half a battalion of gallant British troops was destroyed, but the American attack was blunted and the enemy had time to re-form.

Greene, meanwhile, had pressed forward eagerly to get a nearer view of the field, without observing that there was nothing between him and the enemy but the saplings that grew by the wayside. Major Burnet, his principal aide, saw his danger and warned his chief as Greene was riding full tilt toward the foe. Turning his horse's head, Greene rode slowly back to his own lines.

The moment was trying. Greene had heard nothing from Harry Lee and naturally feared the worst. The enemy was gaining ground again on his right and already had turned the American left flank. This development, Greene felt, justified his distrust of green troops and his decision to save his veteran Continentals. Although at this point Greene had not conquered Cornwallis, he had badly crippled him. The enemy had been severely mauled. So the Amercan objective was attained. Greene would not sacrifice more of his men on the mere chance that the British, as seemed likely, could be overwhelmed. The price in American blood would have been terrific, and he ordered a retreat.

Cornwallis quickly was driven back when he tried to

pursue, in itself evidence that his lordship had no stomach for further fighting. Greene marched back to his old encampment on Troublesome Creek.

Tactically the battle was a victory for Cornwallis, since he held the field. But Greene had achieved his purpose; he had hurt Cornwallis so badly that he would have to retreat to Wilmington, and the result was satisfactory to the Rhode Islander. As some historians assert, Greene said he would "be glad to sell his lordship another field at the same price."

Both sides were forced, because of a hard rain that set in, to leave their dead and wounded out all night. But next day, under a flag of truce, each helped the other bury the dead and care for the wounded.

Cornwallis listed 93 killed and 439 wounded, some of whom later died. Losses were particularly heavy among his officers. Greene lost 300 killed and wounded in the ranks of his Continentals. The militia counted 103 dead and wounded, and in addition 294 were listed as missing. Greene's wry comment was that they had "gone home to their wives and sweethearts." The men simply had vanished. Greene also had lost his fieldpieces to the enemy during his quick retreat. But more important than the ratio of losses in dead and wounded was the fact that, under favorable circumstances, the Americans had proved again that they could stand up and slug it out with the best British troops.

The victory was a hollow one for Cornwallis, as he well knew. Charles James Fox said in England when he heard the news that "another such victory would destroy the British army," but his lordship didn't need Fox or anyone else to tell him so. Horace Walpole said even more plainly the battle indicated ultimate defeat for the British in the war.

Cornwallis's army lay at Guilford Courthouse, on the battlefield, for nearly two days recuperating. Food was scarce, for, even though the army was in Tory country, the populace didn't have the food and forage for Cornwallis. His effective fighting strength was down to 1500 men. He could not put out foraging parties far away from camp, for fear they would be cut up piecemeal by Lee's cavalry. Without supplies, and low on ammunition, Cornwallis would have great difficulty effecting a safe retreat, let alone attacking Greene, who was in good fighting trim, except for his battle losses and heavy desertions.

Two days were enough to convince Cornwallis that he must retreat to Cross Creek on the Cape Fear River, halfway to Wilmington, and hope for Tory recruits and supplies. On March 18 he pulled out of his camp at Guilford Courthouse, leaving seventy wounded under a flag of truce, and headed for the seacoast.

Greene, who had hoped his lordship would turn again and fight, but not expecting he would, followed closely on the British heels, badly harassing the enemy. But when the Americans reached Ramsey's Mills on the Haw River, they discovered that the earl had marched the previous day for Cross Creek.

There Cornwallis quickly discovered that he could get neither Tory recruits nor provender. He had no alternative but to march his weary, footsore, and nearly starving army to Wilmington. Sending word to Colonel Lord Francis Rawdon, his second in command, he asked him to take over in South Carolina, protect the important British posts in that state, and meet whatever opposition might come from Greene. Then the tired, dispirited, and badly decimated British army began the long, dreary march toward Wilmington. Cornwallis arrived at the seaport on April 7.

Greene's fertile mind at once saw the strategic and tactical advantage that Cornwallis, in desperation, had been forced to hand over to the Americans. Overnight the situation had changed.

Nothing lasting could be accomplished by pursuing Cornwallis to the outskirts of Wilmington. His lordship, by his retreat, in effect had abandoned all of North Carolina but that small coastal enclave. The rest of the state virtually was free of British domination. But South Carolina still lay prostrate under an uneasy British heel. The chance Greene had been waiting for had come. By turning south from Ramsey's Mills on the Haw River he could threaten such important British posts as Camden, Charleston, Georgetown, Ninety Six, and Augusta.

True, young Lord Rawdon had some 8000 troops, but

two thirds of them were Tories. And, because he must garrison all of these important posts, Rawdon's effective field strength was reduced to about 1500 men. With the help of such partisans as Marion, Sumter, and others, Greene was sure he would be able to harass the British, if nothing else, and loosen their hold upon the state. He would buy time, and, with reinforcements, later he might be able to reclaim the whole area.

Meanwhile, if the British remained shut up in Wilmington, they could not reclaim North Carolina nor could they help Rawdon. And if Greene's activities succeeded in baiting Cornwallis into a South Carolina venture, that result would suit Greene admirably.

Rawdon's personal command of 1500 troops lay at Camden, where Gates had been so badly beaten. Greene's hard core of 1500 Continentals would be sufficient for the flying corps he had in mind for this South Carolina venture. The Continentals had proved on more than one battlefield that they were a match for the best British troops. He had no fear of putting them again to the test. And he had Marion and Sumter's partisan guerrillas to help.

First of Greene's objectives would be to drive the British out of their posts along the Santee and the Congaree Rivers.

Greene moved on April 6, 1781, from Ramsey's Mills in North Carolina, toward Camden, South Carolina, for a direct confrontation with Lord Rawdon.

# 16

## Hobkirk's Hill

★★★★★★★★★★★★★

Almost the only opposition the British had in South Carolina at the moment came from the hit-and-run attacks of Marion and Sumter.

Greene wrote to Marion: "Spies are the eyes of the army," and that he was "at present badly off for information of the enemy. It is of the highest importance that I get the earliest intelligence of any reinforcements that may arrive at Charleston." Later Greene wrote to Marion of the "great sense I have of your merit and services." Marion, he felt sure, even then, never would let him down.

Of Sumter he was not too sure, but to the Gamecock he wrote: "Reinforcements are coming from the northward, which I hope will enable us to free your state from the savage treatment of the enemy."

The most important British interior posts in South Carolina were Camden, on the Wateree River, farthest north and the strongest; Georgetown, near the mouth of the Pee Dee River; and Ninety Six, so-called because the post was ninety-six miles from Keowee, the principal village of the Cherokee Indians and the place to which the natives for years had been accustomed to go for their yearly gifts from the British, near the sources of the Saluda River. Fort Watson, Fort Granby, Fort Motte, and the post at Orangeburg gave the British a strongly interwoven web of relatively secondary positions.

Lord Rawdon's regular army was strengthened by the addition of highly trained Tory units as well as Tory irregulars and partisans.

That Cornwallis, having retreated to the safety of Wilmington, would be too proud to return to Charleston seemed probable to Greene. In effect, such a move would admit defeat. To march northward into Virginia would give his lordship a chance to redeem himself by conquering that state. Moreover, most of Greene's supplies had been coming from Virginia, as Cornwallis knew. If the British could cut them off, Greene's operations in South Carolina might be blocked. Also American recruits from the North must pass through Virginia.

Greene had expected reinforcements from the North as he told Sumter, but he ordered the Marquis de Lafayette and General (Mad Anthony) Wayne and his Pennsylvanians, who were to have joined the Southern army, to remain for the time being in Virginia. They were to watch, and if necessary, fight Cornwallis if he moved into that state. Meanwhile, Greene himself must be prepared to retreat again over the Dan if Cornwallis unexpectedly should try to outflank the American army in South Carolina. Greene made all his plans for such a retreat, sending Marion and Sumter out on the flanks. Boats were collected on the riverbanks.

Then Greene marched toward Camden, slowly, so as not to exhaust his men under the hot South Carolina sun. His wagons and baggage, together with his invalids, were sent under guard to Salisbury. Lee was ordered to harass Cornwallis and screen the movements of the main army. Greene cautioned the impetuous Lee to "remember that you command men, and that their powers may not keep pace with your ambition."

While Greene lay camped at Lynches River, where Gates had encamped the year before, he learned that Lee and Marion had anticipated the attack on Camden by capturing Fort Watson on the Santee River. This fort was one of the strongest of the British river outposts and particularly vital to the enemy, because it lay about sixty miles from both Charleston and Camden. It was a kind of halfway station, built on an old Indian mound. Cannon ordinarily would have been needed to reduce the post, since it was protected by a strongly built stockade made of pointed logs and a frontal attack would have been suicidal. But the ingenious Lee devised another scheme.

Greene's descent into South Carolina was not yet generally known, so Lee and Marion had been able to invest the garrison of Fort Watson by surprise. At once Lee set his men to work in the woods with axes to cut down tall trees. Soon a huge tower loomed over the fort's ramparts, and the interior was under the fire of Lee's riflemen. The defenders were helpless and could not pour in an enfilading fire at the Americans, when they tore out the stockade, log by log, and gained an open way into the fort. The British were forced to surrender.

Camden had been chosen by the British as their anchor post in South Carolina because of its strong natural position. The town lay on flat land a mile from the heavily pine-forested east bank of the Wateree River. It was covered on the south and southwest by the river and on the east by Pine Tree Creek. These streams formed a continuous line of defense on two sides. In the center was a chain of strong redoubts, or self-contained and connected earthworks, and a stockade. The 900-man regular garrison consisted mostly of well-trained Tories.

Lord Rawdon, then only twenty-six, had risen by sheer ability from the rank of lieutenant at Bunker Hill to that of brigadier general. He was a brilliant leader and enjoyed the full confidence of Lord Cornwallis, whom he resembled in many respects. Rawdon was dashing and bold, something of a gambler in military affairs, and he had complete faith in himself. His position was strong at Camden, and he realized the necessity of keeping it. If Camden fell, the whole system of British forts in South Carolina would be endangered.

Greene, when he came within sight of Camden's fortifications on April 19, decided he could not hope to capture the place by storm without sacrificing too many lives. He had hoped to take Camden by surprise, but Tories had given the alarm and Rawdon was waiting for him. Since Greene's cannon had not yet come up, he was forced to fall back nearly two miles to a strong position on Hobkirk's Hill. There he dug in and waited, expecting the impetuous Rawdon to attack. Meanwhile, he surrounded the town and sent his cavalry to cut off communications. The flanks could not be protected from the British either in Charleston or Ninety Six, for he did not have enough men.

To prevent desertions, rolls were called three times a day. To guard against information reaching the enemy passes were banned. Greene was determined to keep his small army intact, for already a drummer boy had deserted, carrying word to Rawdon that Sumter had not come up, as ordered, that Greene's artillery was far in the rear, that the Americans had been weakened by desertion, and that they lacked food.

Rawdon decided to attack Greene on Hobkirk's Hill

immediately. But while his lordship was preparing for his daring venture, Greene, unknown to the British commander, had managed to bring up his guns. Perhaps the drummer boy had been deliberately encouraged to desert and give Rawdon sufficient misinformation to induce him to attack. No one knows.

Rawdon, under cover of thick woods, hoped to catch Greene by surprise early on the morning of April 25. He sallied out of Camden with 900 British and Tory regulars, militia, and a strong force of cavalry, approaching Hobkirk's Hill from the southeast. The Americans were at breakfast when Rawdon's advance guard drove in Greene's pickets at the foot of the hill. The indomitable Colonel Robert Kirkwood fought a bitter delaying action while Greene quickly threw his men into line of battle on the hillcrest. Williams's Marylanders took the American left, Huger's Virginians the right, with Colonel Washington's dragoons and some North Carolina men as a reserve at the left rear. Then Kirkwood fell back to the left flank of the American position.

Rawdon advanced with his dragoons on the right of his line. Greene's artillery, placed between units of his Continentals, opened a surprising fire with grapeshot just as Rawdon began what he thought was an enveloping movement on both ends of the American line. Greene's Continentals, bayonets fixed, charged down the hill. Then Colonel John Gunby's First Marylanders, holding the center, halted briefly to reply to the British musket fire. This unexpected action caused the entire American line to hesitate, threatening to create a serious gap. Rawdon, quick to take advantage, charged, hitting hard with the bayonet at the First Maryland. These veteran troops, although tried on many battlefields, suddenly broke and ran. The Fifth Maryland followed and panic spread to the right flank. The Fourth Virginia quickly began to run up the hill. One company of the First Maryland and the Delaware Light Infantry of Kirkwood held. The Fifth Virginia was ordered to cover a general withdrawal, and another company of Marylanders tried desperately to protect the three American cannon. Rawdon's dragoons overran them, sabering the gunners down like a thorn thicket under an ax.

For the moment Greene was dismayed by the rout of his veteran Continentals, but he was determined to save not only his army but his precious cannon. Utterly disregarding the pleas of his officers, he galloped into the heaviest musket fire, rallied what men he could, and, "like a captain of Grenadiers," personally led them into the melee of fleeing Americans and attacking British cavalry around the three vitally needed guns. When his men hesitated, Greene jumped from his horse and, with the bridle rein in one hand, seized a cannon's rope and helped to drag the heavy gun out of danger. Greene's voice and his example revived the courage of his gunners. The general shouted for camp guards to help pull the guns farther away from the British dragoons and Rawdon's onrushing, bayonet-thrusting infantrymen.

Colonel Washington's cavalry appeared just in time to dispute the field with the British dragoons. Washington had been off on an expedition of his own, at the British left, and had taken several score of prisoners. At once he detailed troopers to guard the prisoners and personally led a countercharge that quickly drove the enemy cavalry from the field.

His precious guns out of danger, Greene, with the aid of Huger and Williams, rallied the panicked troops. Quickly a new American line was formed at the crest of Hobkirk's Hill. With Washington and Kirkwood holding the British dragoons at bay, all the American wounded were carried safely from the field. Then some of Washington's cavalry horses were hitched to the gun limbers, and the cannon were hauled still farther to the rear. Colonel Washington held fast to the prisoners.

Greene hoped Rawdon would attack again. He was confident that the Marylanders and Virginians, thoroughly ashamed of themselves, would stand and die rather than flee a second time. But Rawdon had had enough. He had lost 38 men killed, and some 220 men were wounded or missing. Greene had lost 19 killed, 115 wounded, and 136 missing. Hobkirk's Hill was not a big battle, but it showed Lord Rawdon that ultimately he probably would find himself holding an untenable position at Camden.

For Rawdon still was in a dangerous position when Greene, seeking food, withdrew on May 3 southwestward across the Wateree. From there the little American army threatened British communications and their line of retreat. Rawdon's supply position was even worse than Greene's and he, like Greene, was having much trouble with desertions. Greene had hanged five men for desertion within as many days.

"We fight, get beat, rise, and fight again." Thus Greene, writing of his campaign to date, summed up his efforts in what might have been the official record of the whole war. Time after time, the Americans seemingly had been beaten. Only, much to the disgust of the British generals, they didn't seem to think so.

Even more important for Rawdon, he was on his own, for Cornwallis finally had made up his mind. On April 24, the day before Hobkirk's Hill, Cornwallis had begun a long march northward into Virginia. Sir Henry Clinton fumed and fretted up in New York when he learned of his lordship's move, but all his ranting could not change the fact.

# 17

## Fort Motte

★★★★★★★★★★★★★

Greene had anticipated Cornwallis's move, but in some ways the British retreat northward only added to his problems. For Cornwallis, cooperating with British forces already in Virginia, might decide to set up a chain of posts across the state. This action could cut the North from the South and hinder the passage of supplies and men.

Should such forts be established before Lafayette's small army in Virginia and that of General Anthony Wayne in Pennsylvania joined Greene, he would be quite as much on his own as Rawdon, even more so, since Rawdon could be reinforced and supplied by sea.

Rawdon, meanwhile, debated whether to try to hold his strong position at Camden, realizing that he was flanked

by the Americans. Especially he had to fear the operations of the South Carolina partisans under Francis
Marion and Thomas Sumter, aided by the dashing and
impetuous Lighthorse Harry Lee. These and other units
constantly were cutting up parties of Tory recruits, capturing supplies and spreading terror among the loyal
subjects of King George.

What Rawdon didn't know was that Sumter had proved
himself to be almost wholly unreliable. High-strung and
arrogant, he was apt to be impetuous, however personally
courageous, and fancied himself to be considerably more
of a strategist and tactician than he really was. The Gamecock was at his best as a lone partisan, but he never learned
to take orders or to coordinate his activities with those of
others.

The wispy Francis Marion was quite a different man—
cooperative, willing, inventive, quick to make the right
decisions, and fast in carrying them out. Most of Marion's
battles had been fought within an irregular triangle
formed by the Pee Dee River, Lynches River, where it
joins the Pee Dee, and the Santee River. The High Hills of
Santee, where Marion's ruined plantation lay, overlooked
this region.

Deep within this triangle, in the vast, all but impenetrable swampland of the Pee Dee and the Santee Rivers,
lay Marion's stronghold, Snow Island. It was a many-
acred savannah, with good water and excellent grazing
land for horses and cattle.

Marion was the man to whom Greene now turned, with Lord Rawdon at bay in Camden. Greene sent the dependable Lee and Marion and the far less dependable Sumter to harry British lines of communication and to keep Rawdon off balance.

So dangerously beset by the enemy were Greene's own lines of communication, maintained by couriers to the north, that he was writing all of his dispatches to Washington in code, giving the commander in chief details of his operations. Greene's code number was 310; that for Cornwallis was 306. Greene kept his superior informed with these reports, but made his own decisions as commander in the field, as Washington desired him to do and as Congress had ordered.

On May 10 Rawdon retreated from Camden. Two days later the important town of Orangeburg on the Edisto River to the southwest fell to the Americans, and on the same day Marion and Lee, besieging Fort Motte, farther north at the confluence of the Congaree and Wateree Rivers, found themselves in a race to effect its capture before Rawdon could arrive to the rescue of the garrison.

The big house of the Motte plantation had been seized long before by the British and fortified so that it was too strong for Marion and Lee to attack without artillery. Time was running out for the Americans. Rawdon's campfires could be seen just across the Congaree. Mrs. Motte, owner of the plantation, had taken refuge in an old farm-house nearby, within the American lines. Marion at last suggested in desperation that the only way the enemy could be driven out of the fortified mansion before Rawdon should come up with reinforcements was to burn the big house. They could do so by setting the roof afire with flaming arrows. Without the slightest hesitation, Mrs. Motte reached above the front doorway of the farm-house and took down a bow and several arrows, handing them silently to the Swamp Fox. Soon the flaming arrows had set fire to the roof of the plantation house and quickly the mansion was in flames. The British garrison was forced to flee, and every man surrendered.

At this point Greene, with half a dozen mounted aides, arrived at the scene. He had decided, as on other occa-sions to "see for himself." Rawdon was much too close—just across the river—to take any chances that Marion and Lee might wait too long and be trapped in their eagerness to capture Fort Motte.

Greene, meeting the pint-sized Marion for the first time, dismounted, strode over to the little brigadier, and pumped his hand enthusiastically. He told the Swamp Fox how highly he esteemed him, and he praised the work of Marion and Lee in capturing the important river post right under the nose of the helpless Rawdon across the Congaree.

Lee was made the van of the army on May 13 and with

Marion marched for Fort Granby, at the confluence of the Congaree and the Saluda Rivers, somewhat to the northwest. Three discharges of the lone fieldpiece that Greene assigned to Lee were enough; Fort Granby's garrison sent up a white flag.

Since Sumter had taken Orangeburg on the Edisto River on May 11, Rawdon began a hasty retreat toward Charleston to avoid being cut off from his main base. Greene ordered Marion to attack the British post at Georgetown, farther up the coast. On the way Marion found time to harry Rawdon as far as Moncks Corner, then hurried east to take the seacost town by surprise. The British garrison abandoned Georgetown May 29, withdrawing along the coast to safety in Charleston.

In one month Greene had captured four important British posts and had forced the evacuation of two others. By May 24 he had taken 850 prisoners, including 50 officers, all of whom he sent north into North Carolina and western Virginia under heavy guard. Except for Charleston, there was only one British outpost left in South Carolina. Ninety Six held out because it had not yet been attacked.

The British post at Augusta, in Georgia, was important, too, and both strongholds had to be reduced before Greene could think of putting Charleston under siege. Taking that well-fortified city, which could be reinforced and supplied by sea, might require considerable time.

# 18

## Ninety Six

★★★★★★★★★★★★★★

At the moment horses—for his comparatively small cavalry units and for the quick transport of mounted riflemen —were the greatest need of Greene's little army. To prepare more men to get to more places where they might be needed faster was vitally necessary.

Lafayette had done his best to supply horses, under Greene's urgent orders, but with little success. The Virginia legislature had passed a law that made impressing good horses for the Continental service difficult for the young French general. Tarleton, riding with Cornwallis, later raided patriot paddocks and took everything in sight, including brood mares and stallions of the finest blood lines, so the patriot breeders might better have sent them to Greene.

Greene turned in desperation to Marion, well knowing that the little brigadier could get favors from the South Carolinians who so greatly admired him. But Marion, stepping out of character for once, hotly declared that supplying horses was not within his power. Choosing to regard Greene's order as impugning his patriotism, he began to sulk. He offered to resign, saying he wanted to go to Philadelphia, where he might obtain at the seat of government an assignment giving him a chance to be of greater help.

Greene, ever the diplomat and coordinator, quickly persuaded Marion that he was badly needed right where he was, and Marion, who probably wanted to think so anyway, agreed that Greene was right.

Then trouble with Sumter came to a head. The Gamecock never had got along too well with the impetuous and sometimes tactless Lee, who, as a Continental, was his superior regardless of military rank. Sumter was particularly angry because Lee had captured Fort Granby, an honor that Sumter mentally had reserved for himself. In fact, he might have had the honor of taking Fort Granby had he not twice chosen instead to go wandering off on what at the moment had seemed more attractive game— shooting up and looting British convoys. Many of his followers, indeed, were more interested in looting than in fighting the British. Greene long had known Sumter's men, including some of the officers, were "a wild and law-less band." But they had been useful as guerrillas, and besides, Sumter's name still was magic in some regions of the state. The bold partisan still could be of some use.

Refusing to accept Sumter's resignation, Greene wrote: "It is unnecesary to tell you how important your services are to the interest and happiness of the country."

That message brought Sumter around, especially since Lee had become the van of the army under Greene's per-sonal command and was no longer fighting independently. This reorganization ended the friction between Lee and Sumter, who was put in titular command of militia in South Carolina as a sop to his vanity. But most of Sumter's usefulness was ended. Greene himself always had re-garded Lee as, "the most brilliant of partisan" leaders, and Lee always cooperated. As events turned out, Greene might have been better off if Sumter's resignation had been accepted.

At last Greene was ready to attack the last two inland British strongholds. Lee was ordered to march with his Legion to Augusta on May 16. He arrived three days later to find Brigadier General Andrew Pickens and Major Jonathan Clark of Virginia already there, as expected. Lee laid siege, building a huge wooden tower from which riflemen could fire into the fort. After days of heavy fight-ing, the garrison of 330 Tory militia and 300 Creek In-dians was forced to surrender on June 6.

Ninety Six was the only area in South Carolina where

the British still held out, save for the district between Moncks Corner and nearby Charleston. Although Rawdon was a flanking peril, Greene pushed on to besiege Ninety Six, just west of the Saluda River. There was danger that Rawdon in a surprise, forced march would cut him off, but he hoped to meet his lordship in open battle before attacking Ninety Six. Rawdon apparently was not yet ready for such an undertaking.

Greene marched through an extremely fertile territory, one that had been ravaged by Whig and Tory alike. It was a healthy region, despite the growing heat. Ninety Six was quite useless to the British since the other forts had fallen, and indeed British Colonel John N. Cruger, commanding, had been instructed to fall back on Augusta. Thanks to Greene's guerrillas, the orders never had reached him. He had a garrison of 350 well-trained Tory riflemen and 50 regulars. The fort was an old stockade, around which the British had built new redoubts. Inside a jail had been fortified, and there was a covered way leading to an ample water supply.

Greene had completely surrounded the town by May 25, and Kosciusko began to build trenches that were dug ever nearer to the British earthworks and from which cannon could pound the redoubts. The British garrison made several surprise sorties, but the Americans drove them back into their own defenses each time they attacked. Then Greene built a tower of green logs, and from the shielded top of this contrivance his men poured a deadly fire into the British works. Fireballs from the fort failed to ignite the green wood. Lee arrived with his dragoons on June 8 from the successful siege of Augusta, and after four days he nearly had cut off the British water supply. Cannon from the main fort was silenced by American riflemen in the tower, and American cannon pounded at the redoubt. A heavy toll had been taken on both sides after eighteen days of the siege.

No one in the American camp apparently thought much about the incident when, on the evening of June 12, a countryman rode almost unchallenged through the American lines. As he neared the open space between the patriot trenches and the British redoubt, he suddenly put spurs to his horse and galloped inside the enemy lines before he could be shot down. Not until much later did Greene learn that the "countryman" was a courier from Rawdon. Cruger was told that his lordship was advancing as fast as the hot weather permitted to raise the siege of Ninety Six.

But Greene had known for six days that Rawdon was marching northwest toward Ninety Six. He had sent orders to Marion and Sumter to delay Rawdon. With Lee's and Washington's dragoons they were to harass the British. Only a few officers of Greene's immediate staff knew that the battle had developed into a race between siege tactics and Rawdon's relief column.

The irresponsible, grumpy Sumter again disobeyed orders. He tarried at Fort Granby, on the Wateree, think-

ing that Rawdon might try to retake that post. Thus
Sumter permitted Rawdon to get between Greene and
himself. Sumter was too weak in manpower to engage
Rawdon alone, and there was too little time to get around
him. Rawdon pushed on for Ninety Six, while Marion,
Lee and Colonel Washington all supposed that Sumter
still was holding his assigned section of the line protecting
Greene's flank.

Greene had only 1000 men to Rawdon's 2000. Nevertheless, he yielded finally to the plea of his men, "give us one
more chance, General. We have a stain to wipe away,"
and reluctantly ordered a general assault on the works at
Ninety Six. It failed, as he had feared it would, with
heavy loss.

Scouts rode in to tell Greene that Rawdon was near.
Soon the little American camp might be caught in a
pincers movement between Rawdon and the defenders
under Cruger. There was only one move to be made—
retreat again—just when victory seemed certain. The
siege had lasted twenty-eight days, and Greene had lost
185 men, killed and wounded. The setback was his first
since opening his South Carolina campaign, and all because the Gamecock once again had disobeyed orders.

Some of Greene's officers urged him to fall back again
across the Dan River into Virginia. This line of retreat still
was open if he could keep ahead of Rawdon.

Greene snorted in disgust at the suggestion, shook his

head, and tightened his lips into a thin line. With a hard expression in his usually amiable blue eyes, he announced, "I will recover South Carolina, gentlemen, or die in the attempt!" There was no further argument. Greene began his forced retreat, but not to the Dan.

Pushing his men well ahead of Rawdon, Greene headed for the High Hills of Santee. He was not only disgusted with Sumter, he was wrathful with Governor Jefferson of Virginia for holding back supplies, especially horses, from the army in South Carolina. His men were subsisting much of the time on rice and cooked frogs.

More than ever Greene longed for his beloved Caty, whom he had not seen for such a long time. When the military situation should become more stabilized he would send for her, but South Carolina still was much too dangerous a spot for her.

So Greene girded for new trials, confident of ultimate victory at the end of his one-sided struggle against superior forces. His will was as resolute as ever, his stout heart as courageous, and his strenuous exertions never relaxed. The pace he maintained, from before daylight on many mornings to the small hours of the night when his last report or letter had been written, would have undermined the health of many men. Indeed, he was not wholly well, for he still suffered from attacks of asthma. But the pure, clear air of the high hills was invigorating.

Greene tightened up discipline. His order of the day on

July 16 emphasized the need for personal cleanliness
among the men. They were to exercise daily by companies, and occasionally there were to be brigade exer-
cises in the cool of the late afternoon. The roll was
called four times daily to guard against desertions. There
was a daily parade and strict guard duty. Careful watch
was kept on the health of the prisoners, with reports to
Greene in writing from the doctors. Otho Williams proved
to be an excellent adjutant general and inspector general,
and he saw that clothing and arms were kept in good
order. Soon more horses were driven into camp, and
Greene had more mounted men for scout duty and quick
forays on the enemy below the hills. The general cracked
down severely on the growing tendency to rob both Whig
and Tory in the lowlands. He was particularly emphatic
in orders to General Pickens, being "exceedingly disturbed that the practice of plundering still continued to
rage." The Tories, he pointed out, must be encouraged to
return with confidence to their homes, for they would be
needed to farm the country when peace was restored.
Colonel Wade Hampton, a dashing new arrival from
South Carolina, was ordered to bring in captured plun-
derers to be tried by a military court, but Greene shared
the longing of South Carolinians generally for a quick
return to civil law.

"I am not fit for a military life," he wrote, "for I cannot
adopt its maxims."

# 19

## The High Hills of Santee

★★★★★★★★★★★★★★

Rawdon's men were dropping dead from exhaustion and
heat in their hot pursuit of the Americans through the
steaming lowlands and over marshy rivers. Soon Rawdon
was forced to head back to Charleston, for he, too, was
running short of provisions in this richly fertile but war-
ravaged land.

Conditions for Greene's little army were pleasant and
comparatively safe in the High Hills of Santee, a long,
irregular chain of hills northeast of Charleston. The hills
consist of huge masses of sand, clay, and gravel, some
twenty-four miles long, rising two hundred feet above the
riverbanks. The climate was healthy on this fertile pla-

teau, and the water was pure. The region was an oasis in
the wide tract of miasmic and fever-ridden land in which
the American army had been operating.

Officers and men badly needed the rest. Greene could
reorganize and await recruits and supplies from the
North, leaving Marion and Sumter to guard his flanks. But
Sumter again was proving wholly unreliable, and most of
the scouting fell upon Marion and Lee, with help from
Colonel Washington and Colonel Hampton, who was one
of Marion's best partisan officers.

Greene's inventive mind was always at work. When he
learned definitely that Cornwallis had committed his
army to action in Virginia, abandoning the rest of the
South, he wrote to Washington on June 22 that the British
in Virginia were within the power of the American Army
"if the French fleet with a large land force should enter
Chesapeake Bay." This advice was not the first strategic
or tactical idea that Washington had received from his
most trusted lieutenant. And some authorities agree that
the timely suggestion ultimately influenced Washington's
decision to trap Cornwallis by just such a pincers move.
Greene estimated that the British in Virginia might be
forced to surrender in three weeks or less. Charleston or
New York, he said, would require longer to subdue.

During this time Greene received some sad news. Word
came from the North that his favorite brother, Colonel
Christopher Greene, had been killed in May at his post in
Croton, New York.

Governor Rutledge, at Greene's urgent invitation, returned to South Carolina from long exile and set up a skeleton civil government in the military camp of his close friend in the high hills. Rutledge's first acts were a proclamation against plundering and a call upon all civil officers to enforce the laws, using the state militia.

Reading reports was the hardest chore of the day for Greene. Most of them were written on coarse, dingy paper —in the bad penmanship and "clublike hand" of Otho Williams; the bold style of Harry Lee, "dashing over the pages with the swift impulse of a saber stroke"; and the "elaborate flourish" of Francis Marion. There was Sumter's "elaborate signature," which always brought a smile to Greene's generous lips. How important the Gamecock considered himself! Andrew Pickens wrote in a "tone of higher culture," while there was the "cautious habit of the pen" that indicated the writer as William Davie. William Washington wrote with a "delicate movement of the pen, like the touch of a gentle maiden," belying the fact that his swift saber stroke meant instant death to a foe.

During the nearly two months the army rested in the High Hills of Santee, Greene had to be tough. He hanged men who deserted. He dismissed officers who were found guilty of gross irregularities or insubordination. When the British in Charleston hanged Colonel Isaac Hayne, a South Carolina patriot officer who had been paroled and later refused to serve in the king's Army, Greene was in the most towering rage any man had beheld and threat-

ened to retaliate against any British Tory officers who
might fall into his hands. He never carried out this
threat.

Sumter's band captured 700 British gold guineas on one
daring raid. Instead of turning over the badly needed
money to Greene so he could buy clothing for the whole
army, Sumter divided the booty among his own men.
Then he disbanded the brigade, contrary to orders. Colonel John Henderson was given the task of restoring some
semblance of order below the hills. Greene's orders to
Henderson were: "Punish plundering with the utmost
severity."

For the most part, Greene was forced to operate without knowing what was happening from day to day in the
northern theater of war. Technically his command extended from Delaware to Georgia, but communication
with his far removed subordinates was irregular and un-
safe. He still wrote dispatches in cipher. Lafayette and
Baron von Steuben, operating in Virginia, were supposed
to be a part of Greene's Southern command, but he heard
from them infrequently.

Lord Rawdon went home during the summer to En-
gland to recuperate from an illness. Lieutenant Colonel
Duncan Stewart succeeded to the British command in
South Carolina. Cornwallis already was at Yorktown.

Stewart hastened to take the field and made camp near
the end of August at the junction of the Wateree and

Congaree Rivers while Greene's army still occupied the High Hills of Santee. As the crow flies, the two armies were only some sixteen miles apart, but a vast network of impassable swamps separated them. The riverbanks were overflowing from heavy rains, and the surrounding lowland country was like a vast, swollen lake. Trees rose majestically from the water, with pendant moss hanging from their branches like the whiskers of very old men. Vast tracts of cane waved in the swift current.

When Greene marched on August 22, 1781, determined to eliminate the last British field force in South Carolina, he was obliged to make a seventy-mile detour to reach the enemy. The marching was hard, for the days were hot and sticky in the lowlands. Greene moved only during the early morning and late afternoon, resting his men during the hottest hours. They must be fresh and strong when they reached the vicinity of Stewart's army. The Americans numbered 2600 men, of whom only 1600 were "effectives"—men who were fit for first-line duty. Stewart had about 2000 men, but nearly all of them were first-line troops, and he had three fieldpieces.

Six days later, on August 28, Greene camped at Motte's plantation on the Congaree, near the site of old Fort Motte. Stewart fell back toward Eutaw Springs on the Santee River. Keeping only two wagons for hospital stores and rum for the men, Greene sent back his baggage on a safe line of retreat. His slow and easy marches were not wholly to keep his men rested; he also wanted to cover his intentions and to give Marion time to join him.

Marion returned, on August 30, "radiant with success" from a special expedition to Parker's Ferry. There his partisans had defeated a band of 300 British and Hessians, 80 dragoons, and a body of Tories, killing 20, wounding 80, and capturing 40 horses. Marion lost 4 killed and wounded. The raid was another of the little brigadier's daring and successful hit-and-run missions that helped greatly to keep the British off balance.

Vigilant American patrols cut off Stewart's couriers so that he was without exact intelligence concerning Greene's movements. Marion's men, working through the swamps, continued to harry the enemy as Stewart encamped at Eutaw Springs.

The night of September 7 Greene, unknown to the enemy, camped only seven miles from Stewart.

# 20

## Eutaw Springs

★★★★★★★★★★★★★★

Despite the occasional harassment of his flanks, Stewart felt secure at Eutaw Springs, for it was an ideal spot to defend if Greene gave battle. On the right was Eutaw Creek, which issued from a deep ravine and ran under high banks, thickly bordered with brush and underwood. The only open ground was a large field that had been cleared of timber on both sides of the road. It was commanded by a brick house, two stories high, with garret windows, making a third story, and walls strong enough to withstand light artillery.

In back of the house there was a garden, surrounded by a strong palisade, which covered the space between it and Eutaw Creek. A barn and smaller buildings afforded good rallying points. The approach to the rear was cut up by springs and deep hollows and an almost impenetrable thicket of blackjack, a local shrub. On every side the woods came down in dark masses to the border of the clearing.

Midway through the clearing, and dividing it into almost equal parts, a recently opened road forked directly in front of the house and garden, and about fifty yards from them, it formed two branches. One led to Charleston and the other to a plantation on the Santee. The British camp lay in the field under cover of the house, on both sides of the road.

Greene was in the saddle well before dawn on the morning of September 8, 1781. The day turned bright and clear, with a cloudless sky, and already the sun was hot. The road to Eutaw Springs was heavily wooded, which was good. The growth gave protection against both the enemy and the heat.

As Greene's spirited charger pranced skittishly along, a dust-covered courier rode in from the North with a dispatch. Greene tore open the seal, and a smile of thankfulness softened the stern lines of his mouth. The message was from George Washington and told him that the commander in chief and the Count de Rochambeau, with almost the entire army of the North and 5000 veteran French troops, were on a forced march southward through the Jerseys to invest Cornwallis at Yorktown, Virginia.

Equally important, a powerful French fleet under Admiral Count François J.P. de Grasse at that very moment was sailing up from the West Indies to Chesapeake Bay. There de Grasse would rendezvous with a smaller fleet and French troops from Newport, Rhode Island, under Admiral de Barras. The combined forces would lay siege to the British on the Yorktown peninsula, from which there would be no escape. Only a stronger British fleet could rescue Cornwallis now, and, for the moment, the French naval strength in North America was greater than that of the British.

This plan was the very one that Greene had proposed much earlier to Washington, and he often had speculated over its execution. For success of such a venture depended upon Admiral de Grasse, and only recently had events combined to make possible such a daring combined allied operation by land and sea. Washington and Rochambeau were joining forces with Lafayette in Virginia, and Washington was taking personal command as allied commander in chief.

Greene had no time for more than a brief feeling of exultation. It was eight o'clock, and the two American columns were within four miles of Eutaw Springs. He needed to concentrate on what lay ahead, for at any minute the enemy might be expected to discover the approach of his army, and the battle would be joined.

Almost upon the instant, a courier from Lee, scouting well ahead of the main body, informed Greene that an advance party of the enemy cavalry had been sighted. Commanded by Major John Coffin, it had been sent out on a scouting expedition. Lee at once deployed his Legion across the road and sent Colonel John Henderson and his sharpshooting militiamen into a thicket at one side.

Soon, above the din of firing up ahead, Greene detected the sound of General John Armstrong's advance guard galloping back toward the main American army. They were closely pursued by Coffin's troopers, charging at headlong speed. Coffin thought he was fighting militiamen. But, instead of continuing to run, Armstrong's men turned and poured in a deadly fire. Empty saddles appeared in the British ranks. Then, as the enemy fell into disorder, the infantrymen of Lee's Legion charged with the bayonet and its cavalry quickly gained the rear, cutting the enemy off. Breaking under the double shock, the foe ran, every man for himself, fleeing into the woods. Forty were taken prisoner.

Stewart had sent Major Coffin forward to investigate a report brought in earlier by two American deserters, telling him that Greene was marching on Eutaw Springs. Still earlier Stewart had been disturbed because some men of his "rooting parties," sent out by the commissary department to dig sweet potatoes, had failed to return. Reluctantly he came to the conclusion that they had been captured but whether by Greene's men or partisans under Marion or Pickens he could not be certain.

At this point Greene personally cantered forward to-

ward the sound of firing up front. Soon he was in the
midst of the wild tangle of wounded and dying men,
screaming, plunging horses, and the thick, acrid smoke of
musket fire. As usual, in utter disregard for his own safety,
he wanted to see what was happening for himself.

He was trying to sort out the action when an aide galloped up and reported, "General Greene, sir, there is a
large body of the enemy in your rear!"

Greene, without turning his head, replied, "Ride up to
them, sir, and tell them that if they do not immediately
surrender, I shall be under the necessity of cutting them
to pieces with the horse!"

The aide carried the message. The British, completely
cut off, quickly surrendered. Greene went about his business, making further battle arrangements.

Greene deployed his two columns in battle lines similar
to those used at Cowpens and Guilford Courthouse. The
militia was placed in the front line. The center he gave to
the most reliable of these units, one from North Carolina
under Colonel the Marquis de Malmedy, a French volunteer officer. These men were flanked on the right by
Marion's South Carolina partisans and on the left by
South Carolina partisans under Pickens.

The right of the second line consisted of a newly raised
North Carolina Continental brigade under General Jethro
Sumner. In the center were Virginia Continentals commanded by Lieutenant Colonel Richard Campbell, and on
the left were the "old reliables," Colonel Otho Williams's

Maryland brigade. Lee's Legion, both cavalry and infantry, protected the right flank, while on the left flank were South Carolina infantry under Henderson and cavalry commanded by Wade Hampton. Greene held William Washington's always dependable dragoons and Colonel Robert Kirkwood's Delaware Continental infantry in reserve.

Stewart had drawn up his men in a single line, thinking that his veterans easily could defeat American troops, most of whom were militia. Guarding the right flank, near the banks of Eutaw Creek, were regular light infantry and Grenadiers. The left flank was protected only by some 50 cavalrymen and 150 infantry under Major Coffin. These men served not only as a flank guard, but as Stewart's single reserve. While he was making belated but hasty preparations for a battle he had not expected to fight, he sent a contingent of Tories ahead to delay the Americans. Stewart's intelligence had been very bad, since his couriers and spies had been intercepted by Marion and Pickens, operating from nearby swamps.

Greene sent his fieldpieces forward at a gallop. Quickly unlimbered, they began to pound the enemy hard, most of the shots tearing wide holes in the British front. The first American line followed fiercely on the heels of the cannoneers. Lee on the right and Henderson on the left fired obliquely as they moved out at an angle on the flanks.

Quickly the British van was driven in. Stewart, seeing

none but militia before him, exhorted his troops, "Hold firm, my men! Drive them back without leaving your ground!"

But on this day the militia were led by Francis Marion and Andy Pickens, and they were not to be frightened by British bayonets. They felt like veterans. Artillery on both sides was in full play. Even when both of Greene's cannon were disabled, the American first line stood firmly against the weight of the whole British army. Then a British cannon was put out of action, cutting down the heavy enemy fire. The militiamen were steady, firing low, where they could do the most damage. They also shot accurately, with the fearful precision that daily practice gives to the hunter's aim. Deep, regular volleys of British musketry answered. These men, too, were firing with precision, but with almost no true aim.

Still the unwavering militiamen held their ground while the British line kept up its fire. On the right, the infantry of Lee's Legion engaged the British steadfastly; on the left, Henderson's men took a galling fire without retreating. In this sector the British were secure behind a thicket in Eutaw Gardens. Henderson gladly would have charged with the bayonet, but he knew he must hold the flank. His men were unflinching.

But the situation rapidly was worsening in the center of the American first line. Untrained militia were pitted against the steady, trained persistence of the British infantry. The enemy charged again with the bayonet, and the militia gave ground, but not until every man had fired seventeen rounds.

Although Jethro Sumner's corps was filled with raw recruits, he charged handsomely into action to fill the gap, bolstering Lee and Henderson. Greene was holding back the battalions of Otho Williams and John Eager Howard to strengthen his main line for the final struggle. The conflict became fully pressed. Then the enemy, too, wincing at last under the deadly fire of the Americans, was forced back.

Stewart, having formed but one line of redcoats in the confident expectation he quickly could shatter this army of ragamuffins and country bumpkins, must have had some second thoughts at this point. The moment was a critical one for him, and he had no time for second guessing. Greene's second line and all of his cavalry were in reserve, fresh for renewed fighting. Stewart threw his scanty reserves into action, ordering Major Coffin to take post on his left where open ground exposed the British to a charge by the American cavalry. Thus condensed, and feeling the effects of the fresh support, the British lines bore up nobly against the American fire.

Then Henderson on the American left was wounded. For a moment his men wavered as their leader reluctantly left the field, but the impetuous and gallant Wade Hampton promptly took over command. He put himself at their head, quickly restoring order. Sumner's brigade had stiffened the American center line, fighting with the calm coolness and resolution of veterans. The whole American front surged forward, forcing the British slowly but surely backward.

Still, the reinforced British line was the stronger and soon, after fierce and obstinate resistance, the American center was compelled again to retire. Sumner held his men in front of the bruising fire as long as he could. With loud shouts, sensing victory, the British center returned to the charge. And so eager was the enemy to rush in for the kill that their line quickly became disorganized.

This was the moment that Greene had been waiting for. His sharp eye caught the surge of red uniforms bending his own center line taut like a bowstring ready for the flight of an arrow.

Campbell's brigade of Virginia Continentals and Williams's Marylanders were ordered forward on the double, arms trailed, holding their fire and pressing hard against the British line with fixed bayonets. The Virginians and Marylanders charged with a loud, confident shout that could be heard above the tumult of the battlefield. Soon their line extended beyond the British left.

Quickly Lee ordered a detachment to pour in a raking fire to turn the enemy flank. The main body of Marylanders, obeying orders, charged with cold steel without pulling a trigger. But the Virginians, less trained for such a desperate struggle, returned the enemy's fire, endangering the Legion infantry. Lee galloped back to see what had happened and reached Colonel Campbell just as that gallant officer was cut down with a musket ball. Lee's orderly was told to take Campbell from the field; then Lee rode back to his own men. By that time the enemy's left flank had been turned by his infantry. The Americans were bearing all but one sector of the British line before them. These veterans returned thrust for thrust until many on both sides had fallen. Then the Americans opened fire and forced the thinned-out enemy ranks to break and flee under the double impact of bayonet and bullet. The British rout was complete. The enemy fled through the woods, and some down the Charleston road. Staff officers broke open their stores and stove in their rum puncheons. They were not going to leave more loot than they must to the Americans.

The battle seemed to have been won by Greene's men, but not quite.

The Americans hotly pursued the fleeing British, managing to keep order in their ranks. Soon they were within the abandoned British camp. An abundance of food and drink was within easy reach, and Greene's men were hungry, tired, and thirsty. Tempted beyond endurance, they broke ranks to enjoy the fruits of victory, gorging themselves on the half-eaten British breakfast and drinking the abandoned rum. Then they scattered among the tents in search of more food and drink. A few, including the infantrymen of Lee's Legion, managed to resist temptation and pressed on through the camp, hard on the heels of the British, taking prisoners at every step.

Stewart had not quite realized until this moment how well he had done in choosing this spot as a battlefield. Directly in front of his fleeing troops was the big brick house. One detachment of his men was holed up in the thick-walled structure, with the Continentals close upon them. From the upper stories the British poured down a damaging fire upon the Americans, and even the veteran Continentals were forced to retire to seek shelter.

On the British right, the troops still fought on, partly protected by a thicket. Colonel Washington had overshot a charge against the British when the enemy's left flank and center broke. He was unable to pierce the thicket with his cavalry, and his horse was shot from under him. Several of his officers were brought down by enemy fire, and while Washington was struggling to free himself from his stirrups he was captured.

Kirkwood's Delaware men and Hampton's mounted command came up as the British right flank retreated to the house. Stewart, thus bolstered, tried to renew the battle. Greene brought up his artillery to batter down the house, but to no avail. It was too solidly built.

At this point Major Coffin's cavalry, which had taken post in the field west of the Charleston road, charged those of the Americans who still were scattered among the British tents. Lee's Legion countered, but Coffin forced his way through the disorganized Americans on the camp-site.

Then Wade Hampton galloped up, forcing Coffin's men into a hand-to-hand, mounted saber duel and obliged the British cavalry to fall back to the house for cover. When Hampton retired to the woods to reorganize, the British seized Greene's artillery and dragged it off in triumph. All the gunners had been killed or wounded. Then, returning to the charge, the enemy drove before him the scattered, scavenging American troops, cutting and slashing with heavy cavalry sabers.

The British line by this time was wholly re-formed, thanks to the energy of Stewart and his remaining officers. They were prepared to snatch from Greene what certainly would have been a devastating victory had it not been for the greed, hunger, and thirst of some of his men who had stopped to ransack the British camp.

Greene, riding in front on the right with Lee, had sup-posed, until too late, that the men of the left and center still were rolling up the British line. When he discovered that hundreds of his men had broken ranks and were loot-ing the British camp, he bent all of his efforts to restoring order. With the help of staff officers, he was successful in rallying his men. Then he took a stand on the border of the wood. There he might hope to renew the battle if

Stewart pressed him. But, as at Guilford Courthouse, Greene realized that he had accomplished his major objective, despite the greed of some of his men who had thrown away a sure chance of complete victory.

Stewart certainly had suffered so severly that he could not hope to keep the field. In fact, he had lost forty percent of his army and was forced to retreat to Charleston with all speed. Once cooped up in that seacoast town he could be besieged. And Greene did not believe, in view of the momentous news that had reached him as he marched toward Eutaw Springs that bright morning of September 8, that Stewart would get reinforcements by sea.

Greene's immediate concern, however, was for the safety of his army and the care of his wounded. This bitterly fought battle had cost him 139 killed and 375 wounded. Eight were missing. Stewart had lost 85 killed, 351 wounded, and 430 missing, most of them prisoners.

The engagement was a drawn battle and is rated as the most hotly fought of the war. When, the next day, Stewart retreated to Charleston, leaving seventy of his wounded under a flag of truce to be cared for by the Americans, he scarcely could claim a victory. For all practical purposes, Eutaw Springs was the end of Greene's campaign in the South. Sending Lee and Marion to watch Stewart and to harry his rear guard, Greene again pulled back to the High Hills of Santee.

That night Greene wrote to Washington that Charleston could be taken in the same way as he proposed to capture Yorktown, if Admiral de Grasse could be persuaded to stop off at the Carolina coast on his way back to the West Indies. In any event, Greene wrote to his chief, he would be glad to take part in such a venture, "either as principal or subordinate," that is, either as commander in a joint operation with de Grasse against Charleston, or as subordinate to Washington if the commander in chief cared to move farther south and invest Charleston. Such was the measure of Greene's deep humility. With Washington in the South, he was ready and quite willing to yield his own command, foregoing, if necessary, the honor and glory of the victories he already had won on his own initiative.

# 21

## Greene's Sacrifice

★★★★★★★★★★★★★★

Events had been moving even faster in the North than
Greene had dared to hope. Washington put Yorktown
under siege, using the combined French and American
forces. Cornwallis was trapped. He held out from September 30 to October 19, undergoing hard fighting and a
terrific bombardment, then surrendered. His British and
Hessian army marched out of the town, flags furled, between double ranks of jubilant French and American
troops, to the tune of "The World Turned Upside Down."

One month after the surrender of Cornwallis at Yorktown, Greene, still commanding the Southern army,
struck his tents for the last time at the pleasant camp in

the High Hills of Santee. The army still lacked most of the supplies it needed, but by November 18 Greene was determined to clean up the last pockets of British resistance. Eventually, after sporadic fighting, he bottled up Major General Alexander Leslie, who had succeeded Stewart, in Charleston. This tactic was a calculated risk, because Leslie still might be reinforced by sea. And Greene had learned that he would get little real help from the North and none from de Grasse's French fleet.

"I have not been frightened," Greene wrote when he finally was certain that Leslie would not get reinforcements, "but I have been confoundedly scared."

He sent Anthony Wayne, who had been fighting with Lafayette in Virginia, to free Georgia on January 4, 1782, after Major General Arthur St. Clair had arrived to reinforce the Southern army. Wayne did a brilliant job, although once he narrowly escaped annihilation in a surprise Indian attack.

As the months dragged by, Charleston still lay under siege. Caty Greene arrived in the American camp at the Round O Ranch, several miles outside of Charleston, late in March, 1782, after a long journey from Rhode Island. She was escorted by a small group of officers personally chosen by George Washington. The ride had been gruelling, but she quickly recovered and soon entered with her usual high spirits into the life of the military community.

Even though he was frustrated by shortages of men,

ammunition, uniform clothing, and food, Greene quickly found that life had taken on new zest and meaning. For Caty soon was the center of what social life was possible in the camp and on those neighboring plantations that still could offer hospitality after going through the devastating ravages of war. Some of the other officers' wives joined their husbands for the duration of the Charleston siege. Caty made many friends among the mothers and daughters of neighboring planters, some of whose relatives still were serving with Washington in the North, and others of whom were in Greene's army.

Caty was popular not only with the women but with the officers, too. She rode horseback with the general in the lush countryside. She was gay, although not always in the best of health. "They call her the first lady of Charleston," Greene proudly wrote home. But equally important, the men in the ranks soon learned that Caty Greene, with her hardy Block Island upbringing, was "real army." Often in the hospitals helping the sick, she won their highest respect and admiration, and was the main reason for the sudden uplift in the morale of the little army.

In June, 1782, General Leslie made overtures for an armistice. Greene summarily refused the request. He would accept no terms except surrender and the immediate evacuation of Charleston. The British held on, even though, for all practical purposes, the war was ended. Leslie, a humane and equitable man, felt a high degree of

responsibility for the property and safety of the Tories in
Charleston and sought to make certain that they would
not suffer after he had gone.

In August Greene wrote that one third of his men were
"entirely naked." Wearing a breechcloth only, they never
dared leave their tents, and the rest were "as ragged as
wolves." Clothing was so scarce that some men had to
give up shouldering a heavy musket, because the weapon
bruised bare skin and caused sores. Their provisions were
only a little better, despite the fertile country in which
they lived, for the natives were more demanding in their
prices. They wanted hard money, or gold, for food they
sold to the army. The soldiers often were forced to go
without meat, and the beef they were served was "like
carrion."

Nevertheless, "the army is very contented and easy,
especially since we have it now in our power to issue rum
eight times a month," Greene reported.

No wonder Robert Morris, the Philadelphia financier
and patriot, wrote of Greene: "An officer who finds his
own genius ample resource for the want of men, money,
clothes, arms, and supplies."

The Northern army was fed and clothed on contract,
but the Southern army at this time had to depend upon
the states, and most of them failed to carry out their
agreements with Greene. So the burden fell on South
Carolina. Even Wayne in Georgia had to depend upon

South Carolina for supplies. The only luxuries available to the men were rum and tobacco. Private citizens with limited supplies traded with the British in Charleston, from whom they could get gold for their goods. The contraband trade grew even more profitable as black-market prices soared. Greene summarily rejected a British offer to trade rice for tobacco.

Then John Banks appeared. Banks was at once a merchant, a speculator, and a black-market operator, associated with the otherwise respectable mercantile firm of Banks and Hunter in Fredericksburg, Virginia. Banks offered, for a high price, to supply Greene with most of what the army needed. In return he asked for a safe-conduct pass through the encircling American lines to trade in Charleston. Greene ignored him.

Months dragged by. Mutiny was rumored in the American camp as conditions grew worse. British secret agents stirred the men up still more. Then one day a camp woman told Greene of a plot against him. A body of British cavalry was to wait outside the American camp while on a certain night a picked group of mutineers would seize the general and his chief officers and turn them over to the British. The woman named the ringleaders.

Greene moved fast. The plotters were arrested, put on trial, convicted, and hanged before the whole army. Greene wrote to Otho Williams, who had been invalided home to recuperate from an illness: "This decisive step put a stop to it, and you cannot conceive what a change it has made in the temper of the army."

Yet Green realized that his men literally were starving and many went naked while great numbers of the South Carolinians were trading with the British in Charleston for gold. He protested to his friend Governor John Mathews regarding this "infamous traffic," conducted by "the persons who will contribute nothing for the army because they can get an enormous price and cash for what they send to town," but trading with the enemy still went on.

Dysentery broke out in the American camp. Foraging, even when provisions were taken by force, yielded only a scant supply of food. Greene had authority to procure provisions and clothing, but no money to pay for them. His friend, General Benjamin Lincoln, had been appointed secretary of war, a post Greene himself had turned down to remain with his southern command. Lincoln tried to help, but his department had no money except worthless Continental currency.

Greene was desperate. He had to keep his army together or all that had been won might be lost. Peace negotiations were in progress in Paris, but the British still held Charleston. There was no assurance that the war would not continue indefinitely. The American army had to hold on.

Reluctantly at last Greene sent for Banks, whom he

never had met. In the American camp was George Abbott Hall, a secret agent of Robert Morris, who had gold that had been sent south for the army's use in dire emergency. But even so, only after much argument did Hall reluctantly agree to advance 700 guineas to Banks as part payment for the clothing that he could procure in Charleston on the black market. Soon Anthony Wayne, who had returned in triumph from Georgia, wrote: "The army is better clothed than I ever saw an American army before."

Still there was starvation in the American camp. Again came the eager Banks. He could supply food for the army, he assured Greene, and after much haggling Banks agreed to cut his price. But this time Banks overextended himself. His creditors were pressing, and they agreed to let up on him only if the general personally would guarantee payment. Otherwise there would be no more food for the army.

The decision was trying for Greene. South Carolina had given him a gift of 10,000 gold guineas and Boone's Barony, a handsome plantation north of the Edisto River, in gratitude for his services. Georgia had give him 5000 guineas and the Mulberry Grove plantation on the Savannah River. These gifts had brought Greene financial independence, which was important to him because his private investments had turned out badly. Also he had sold out his business in Coventry to his brothers, and so had no way of supporting his four children in Rhode Island. If he pledged his newly acquired wealth to guarantee payment of Banks's bills for army food, he risked financial ruin. But the army looked to Greene for protection. Could he stand by and watch his men starve? If not, he must risk all he possessed to feed the army and keep it intact.

Banks, ever alert to his own interests, secretly had taken Major Robert Burnet, Greene's longtime trusted aide, and Major Robert Forsythe, another aide, as partners. They, too, urged Greene to endorse Banks's promissory notes. The young men were friends of long standing and had Greene's complete confidence, and their advice finally weighed with him. He did not know they were silent partners of John Banks. The danger to the army was obvious; the necessity for immediate action was urgent. Finally Greene signed, knowing that he risked his entire fortune to feed his starving army. He was pledged to pay for the food if Banks did not.

Greene soon learned how dangerous trusting in the honor of a desperate war speculator was. His enemies—and he had some bitter ones—learned of Burnet's and Forsythe's secret connection with Banks before Greene did. At once, they tried to implicate the general in a deal with the black marketeer.

Summarily, when he learned the facts, Greene ordered Banks into camp. Then, in the presence of Wayne and Carrington, his chief of commissary, he forced the merchant to explain the situation. Banks willingly asserted under oath that Greene had done no wrong and that he knew nothing of Burnet's or Forsythe's activity. But even today there are some historians who hint that Greene somehow was at fault. These men conveniently choose to overlook the fact that Greene knowingly risked his entire fortune, and later lost most of it, to keep his men from starving!

# 22

## Charleston Falls

★★★★★★★★★★★★★★

Not until December 14, 1782 did the British finally evacuate Charleston. The surrender was a great day for the
American army.

The men heard the morning gun fired from one of the
British redoubts. Soon English troops began their final
march to the shore to board the 300 vessels sent to transport them to New York or to England.

Wayne, with three hundred infantrymen, eighty of the
Legion cavalry, twenty artillerymen, and two 6-pounder
cannon, was only two hundred yards behind the retreating enemy. Down King Street and through the city gates
the British marched to Godsden's wharf. There small

boats were bobbing alongside. All the troops were aboard ship by eleven o'clock.

Then, at three o'clock in the afternoon, announced by the blare of a trumpet, General Nathanael Greene, mounted on a superb charger and in full Continental uniform, escorted by Governor Mathews of South Carolina, rode to the statehouse through lines of American troops at present arms. General William Moultrie and General Mordecai Gist came next in line, followed by prominent citizens and Greene's principal officers. Behind the soldiers were the populace, most of them wild with joy. The Tories stayed glumly indoors with their windows shuttered. The day was a sad one for them, although they had been told by Leslie that Greene would treat them generously.

There was a brilliant ball that evening. Decorative paper magnolia leaves hung in graceful festoons overhead in the big ballroom, a scheme supervised by Kosciusko. Caty Greene, at her husband's side, was the center of attraction.

The South was won, but both Washington and Greene kept a wary eye on British movements, even though peace was so near. Not until April 30, 1783, did Greene, still on guard in Charleston, learn of the preliminary articles of peace that had been signed the previous November 30 in Paris. By July, 1783, all his troops were on their way home. Caty went north by ship, for the long overland journey to South Carolina the year before had been too much of a strain for her.

Greene himself followed soon afterward, making the journey on horseback, stopping at cities and towns along the way to accept the homage of the citizenry. In Philadelphia he visited for a last time with George Washington, his friend and former commander in chief. The trip was a triumphal procession for the hero of the Carolinas and Georgia. He was not completely happy, however, until he rode into the yard of his home in Coventry and for the first time saw Caty and their four children together.

There was a big celebration in East Greenwich in Greene's honor. The Kentish Guards, which had supplied more than 30 officers to the Revolution during eight years of war, turned out on parade in smart new uniforms. Cannon boomed, and martial music blared under the stately elms along Main Street. The General Assembly, which sat sometimes in Providence, or Newport, or East Greenwich, came down to Kent County, meeting in grand committee in the courthouse to pay special honor to the state's most distinguished son.

Nathanael Greene wanted nothing more than to enjoy life for a brief spell in Coventry and in Potowomut, his boyhood home. Nonetheless, he was restless and worried. He had come out of the war a poor man, except for the money and the plantations given to him by the legislatures of South Carolina and Georgia. These big holdings, if they could be profitably worked with their slave labor, would make him affluent again. The trouble was that he detested the conditions under which the plantations would have to be run.

"As for slavery," Greene said, "nothing can be said in its defense." He determined to admit his "inherited" slaves to the rights of "copyholders," that is, under an old English law, they would have a permanent tenure or right to a part of the land on which they labored. This land they could work for their own advantage and profit. Death prevented Greene from carrying out this plan fully, but he did for the slaves all he could except to grant them outright freedom. He did not believe his people were ready for that step.

# 23

## Taps for a Hero
★ ★ ★ ★ ★ ★ ★ ★ ★ ★ ★ ★ ★ ★

In the summer of 1784 Greene returned to South Carolina, ready to begin the reconstruction of Boone's Barony and, later, Mulberry Grove, in Georgia. Then he learned that John Banks had gone bankrupt for $150,000 and that the creditors were coming to him for payment.

Banks fled far into the interior. At once Greene ordered his favorite horse saddled, shoved two loaded pistols into leather holsters, and set out alone, on what proved to be a 400-mile journey, looking for the bankrupt merchant. Greene was more wrought up than anyone ever had seen him, fired by a cold, implacable anger that would brook no settlement save what he could exact from Banks. Perhaps he suspected Banks was concealing assets from his creditors and could, in fact, pay them. Such things often happened. Eventually Greene found Banks, but the man was dying and he was penniless. Greene turned his horse's head back toward Boone's Barony, realizing that there was nothing left but to pay Banks's creditors.

He removed the Barony slaves to Mulberry Grove after selling the place and paying his debts. Then he settled down with his family to what he expected would be a routine way of life for many years. The winters would be spent at Mulberry Grove, the summers in a stately house he had bought on Mill Street in Newport. There the cool breezes off the Atlantic would be more healthy for his family than the miasmic summer heat of the Georgia plantation. Once again, with his young children growing up around him, life seemed good. For eight years Nathanael Greene had been away at war, and he was happy at last to settle down to the joys and the problems of peace. He and Washington shared the distinction of being the only general officers to serve for the entire period of the American Revolution.

Again in 1784, as in 1781, Greene was asked to serve as secretary of war, but he declined. He refused a county judgeship in Georgia for the same reason: he was tired of public service for the time. He wanted nothing more than the prospect of a planter's life in Georgia during the long, warm winters and a congenial social life in Newport during the summer. To the Newport home of the Greenes came many famous visitors: Lafayette, who already had asked for the privilege of raising young George Washington Greene and educating him in France should Greene not be able to do so himself; Kosciusko; von Steuben; and many others. The house was gay with laughter, music, and dancing, and Caty was an ever-gracious, popular hostess. Newport was almost like a second home to both of them, and they fitted in as intimately as though they were natives. Frequently Greene and his family sailed up to Potowomut or into beautiful Greenwich Bay and visited his kinsman, William Greene, who later became governor, in the Greene mansion high on the hills in Warwick.

Alexander Hamilton led the fight to induce Congress to pay Greene his expenses in the army, including the funds he lost endorsing John Banks's note. Some time after Greene's death the money was paid finally to his estate.

Greene was elected head of the Society of the Cincinnati in Rhode Island, an organization composed of Washington's officers and others in the Continental Army, but he took almost no part in it. He was offered many civic posts, but declined most of them. Much of his time was spent in writing letters to men of influence in an attempt to right the many wrongs he saw throughout the country. Much of his income was spent in giving financial aid to officers who had served under him.

After a brief rest, his interest turned to political affairs. He shunned public office but his pen was busy with practical suggestions, many of which ultimately took shape in the later organization of the Federal government of the United States. If not an active participant, therefore, in the founding of the Republic, Greene was one of the intellectual godfathers of American democracy, even as he had been the chief and most able strategist, tactician, and organizer in the war for freedom.

He corresponded actively with Washington at Mount Vernon; with Robert Morris in Philadelphia; Governor Joseph Reed of Pennsylvania; Alexander Hamilton, who became the first secretary of the treasury; and many others who were influential in shaping the destiny of the new country.

Most important of Greene's suggestions, and one concerning which he felt deeply, insisting that there could be no compromise on the issue, was that the then existing loose confederation of states was unwieldy and impractical. There should be a union of the thirteen individual states, he said, with a central government having the power to collect its own revenue, thus becoming inde-pendent and commanding respect. This view was directly contrary to those held by many other prominent leaders. They feared a strong central government, and with the experience of the despotic governments of Europe as an object lesson, not without reason. But even at that early period Greene clearly saw, as did some of his friends, that the bickering confederation of states, each weak and jealous of its rights, could not hope to succeed as a strong nation which the others of the world would respect.

Greene said in his letters that a convention should be called to draft a constitution, giving Congress broad powers; that ministers of war and finance should be appointed, with merit the sole qualification for office. He scorned the views of those who were shouting for a dictator to straighten out the fiscal and governmental chaos in which the states were floundering.

But Greene was not universally popular. One Captain Gunn, an officer whom he had been obliged to discipline severely during the Southern campaign, later had married wealth and settled down on a nearby plantation in Georgia. Gunn, whose anger had been smoldering for a long time, finally challenged Greene to a duel. The general declined. He felt that to accept the challenge would be to establish the principle that a subordinate could hold a superior officer personally accountable for acts performed in the line of duty. In this opinion Washington emphatically backed Greene.

Then Captain Gunn sent word that he would attack Greene whenever they met. "Tell him," Greene replied to Gunn's messenger, "that I shall always carry pistols." Greene never heard from Gunn again, and they never met.

In the autumn of 1785 the Greenes gave up their pleasant town house on Mill Street in Newport and became year-round residents of the extensive Mulberry Grove plantation in Georgia. With Louisa, the newest arrival, there now were five children. Neighbors within easy riding distance of Mulberry Grove included General Anthony Wayne, who had become a Georgia planter, too. Captain Nathaniel Pendleton of Virginia, who had been one of Greene's military aides during a part of the Southern campaign, had established himself in Savannah, fourteen miles down the river. Governor Reed of Pennsylvania was proposing, he told Greene, to move the following year and settle in the neighborhood.

Greene quickly adjusted to the life of a Southern planter and apparently enjoyed every hour of the remaining months of his life, except when he had to attend to lingering details of the unfortunate Banks affair. Mulberry Grove was a big plantation, and it had escaped most of the ravages of war. The flower garden was restored to its former beauty, his fields and orchards were in such good shape that, under his personal supervision, they soon would yield better crops than he had dared to hope.

"The prospect," Greene wrote to a friend in the North, "and the house are delightful." He joyed in the fact that he had a "fine smokehouse," a coach house, stables with good riding horses, an outkitchen, and a pigeon house that would accommodate up to one thousand pigeons. He and Caty spent many happy hours riding over the estate and the countryside. Soon the Greenes were as popular with neighboring planters as they had been in Coventry and Newport.

The following spring Greene wrote exultantly that he had "green peas almost fit to eat, and as fine lettuce as you ever saw." He had apples, pears, peaches, apricots, nectarines, plums, figs, pomegranates, and oranges in his orchards. "And we have strawberries which measure three inches around," he added, with pardonable pride.

On June 12, 1786, Greene went to Savannah with Caty to meet one of Banks's creditors for the final settlement of this sad business. They passed the night at the home of Captain Pendleton in Savannah and started home the next day in the cool of the morning, expecting to reach Mulberry Grove well before the day became hot. But Greene's enthusiasm as a planter led him to stop on the way back at a neighboring plantation to examine the rice fields. He spent several hours in this interesting task, but he failed, unlike his host, to carry an umbrella to protect himself from the sun. While he was driving home that afternoon, his head began to ache. Next day the pain was intense, and his forehead was badly swollen. He had suffered a severe sunstroke.

All efforts to save Greene's life failed, and he died a little after daybreak on June 19, 1786.

Anthony Wayne, the hero of the Stony Point and the Georgia campaign, had sat by Greene's bedside most of the week and was the first to break the news to the world. As soon as the arrangements could be made, Nathanael Greene was buried in a vault in a Savannah cemetery with full military honors.

The country mourned him, and Washington offered to educate the Greene's eldest son and his namesake in "either of the genteel professions—at my own expense and charge," but Lafayette already had first claim on that honor. The boy later went to France to live with the Marquis and his family, returning home when the French Revolution broke out. Still later he was drowned and buried beside his father.

Nathanael Greene's military genius stemmed not so much from brilliance as from the possession of good common sense and an ability to make a quick and accurate analysis of a situation. More than any other soldier of the Revolution save Washington, Greene had what all really great soldiers must possess: a sure eye for the swiftly changing scenes of the battlefield, an intuitive sense of what should be done, and the initiative to execute plans without delay. He was a master of the tactics of strategic retreat, as Washington was, and he often saved his army to fight another day. A bolder and less prudent commander might have gambled more, but when the stakes were high enough he dared to risk all.

Greene could be patient with almost every human trait

save stupidity, deliberate disobedience, and disloyalty. His sense of personal honor was equalled only by his insistence on justice and fair play for all. Instinctively he knew how to handle men of differing temperaments, and he had an understanding of the common soldier that even Washington lacked. He possessed the ability to analyze political as well as military trends and the courage to support new ideas publicly.

In addition, Greene had a supreme genius for organization. It enabled him to become an efficient quartermaster general at a time when the fate of the country in large measure depended on his success in supplying the army and moving it. This gift was one of the chief reasons why he later was able to reorganize the Southern army to fight and defeat, in a series of masterly retreats, the heretofore unbeatable Cornwallis, and to free the South from enemy control. His campaign in the Carolinas cleared the way for the surrender of Cornwallis at Yorktown.

Most importantly, perhaps, Greene had a deep reserve of physical and moral courage, and he was a man of intense loyalty, both to personal friends and to Washington. In return he had the loyalty of his own officers and men, with few exceptions, for loyalty begets loyalty.

To no man other than Washington does the United States owe so much as to Nathanael Greene for his military services in the Revolution.

# Bibliography

★★★★★★★★★★★★★★

Alden, John Richard, *The American Revolution: 1775-1783.* New York, Harper, 1954.

———, *The South in the Revolution: 1763-1789.* Baton Rouge, Louisiana State University Press, 1957.

Augur, Helen, *The Secret War of Independence.* New York, Duell, Sloan and Pearce, Inc., 1956.

Bass, Robert D., *The Gamecock: The Life and Campaigns of General Thomas Sumter.* New York, Holt, Rinehart and Winston, 1961.

———, *The Green Dragoon.* New York, Henry Holt and Company, Inc., 1957.

Boyd, Thomas Alexander, *Light-horse Harry Lee.* New

York-London, Charles Scribner's Sons, 1931.

Callahan, North, *Henry Knox: General Washington's General*. New York, Rinehart and Company, Inc., 1958.

Carroll, Dr. Charles, *Your Plantations*. New York, Lewis Historical Publishing Company, 1930.

Clarke, Louise Brownell, *The Greenes of Rhode Island. With Historical Records of English Ancestry, 1534-1902*. Compiled from the mss. of the late George Sears Greene. Vols. I, II. New York, Knickerbocker Press, 1903.

Davis, Burke, *Cowpens-Guilford Courthouse Campaign*. Philadelphia, J. B. Lippincott Company, 1962.

Dean, Sidney W., *Fighting Dan of the Long Rifles*. Philadelphia, Macrae Smith Company, 1942.

Dupuy, R. Ernest and Trevor N., *The Compact History of the Revolutionary War*. New York, Hawthorn Books, Inc., 1963.

Freeman, Douglas Southall, *George Washington*. Vol. IV. New York, Charles Scribner's Sons, 1951.

Frothingham, Thomas G., *Washington, Commander in Chief*. Boston, Houghton Mifflin Company, 1930.

Greene, Francis Vinton, *General Greene*. In the Great Commander Series. New York, D. Appleton and Company, 1893.

Greene, George Washington, *The Life of Nathanael Greene, Major-General in the Army of the Revolution*. Vol. I. New York, G. P. Putnam's Sons, 1867.

———. Vols. II, III. New York and Cambridge, Hurd and Houghton, Riverside Press, 1871.

Headley, Joel Tyler, *Washington and His Generals*. Vols. I, II. New York, Baker and Scribner, 1847.

Heitman, Francis B., *Historical Register of the Officers of the Continental Army During the War of the Revolution, April, 1775 to December, 1783*. Pages 134 and 435. Washington D.C., W. H. Lowdermilk and Company, 1893.

Irving, Washington, *Life of Washington*. Vols. I, II, III, IV. New York, G. P. Putnam's Sons, 1855.

Kurjack, Dennis C., *Hopewell Village, National Historic Site*. Washington D.C., National Park Service Historical Handbook Series No. 8, 1954, 1961.

Lancaster, Bruce, *Phantom Fortress*. Boston, Little Brown and Company, 1950.

Mackesy, Piers, *The War for America, 1775-1783*. Cambridge, Harvard University Press, 1964.

Mahan, Alfred Thayer, *The Influence of Sea-power Upon History, 1660-1783*. Boston, Little Brown and Company, 1890.

Manucy, Albert, *Artillery Through the Ages*. Washington D.C., United States Government Printing Office, 1949.

Pratt, Fletcher, "Nathanael Greene, the Quaker Turenne," *Eleven Generals: Studies in American Command*. New York, William Sloane Associates, 1949.

Providence Institution for Savings, *The Old Stone Bank,*

*History of Rhode Island.* Vol. I. Providence, Prepared and printed by Haley and Sykes, 1929.

Thane, Elswyth, *The Family Quarrel.* New York, Duell, Sloan and Pearce, Inc., 1959.

Thayer, Theodore, "Nathanael Greene, Revolutionary War Strategist." In George Athan Billias, Ed., *George Washington's Generals.* New York, William Morrow and Company, Inc., 1964.

*The National Encyclopedia of American Biography.* Vol. I. New York, James T. White and Company,1898.

Van Doren, Carl Clinton, *Secret History of the American Revolution.* New York, The Viking Press, 1941.

Ward, Christopher, *The War of the Revolution.* Ed. by John Richard Alden. Vols. I, II. New York, The Macmillan Company, 1952.

Westcott, Allan, Ed. *American Sea Power Since 1775.* Philadelphia, J. B. Lippincott Company, 1947.

Willcox, William B., *Portrait of a General: Sir Henry Clinton in the War of Independence.* New York, Alfred A. Knopf, Inc., 1964.

# INDEX